Electric Thunder

Simply Musing

SIMPLY MUSING

Poetry of Life and Love

For Georgia, my own Goddess of the sea, and most beautiful girl in the world

ACKNOWLEDGEMENTS

There are many inspirations for writing poetry. It is seen in the everyday people and situations a poet views. More so you have to acknowledge those close to you for being part of the development of a poet.

With that in mind, I thank the first woman who meant anything to me in my life and has been a source of constant love, support, happiness, sharing in sadness, joy, love and life, my mother Betty. A woman who never relinquishes her role and fulfils it with gusto admirably.

My closest friend and daily companion, my wife, Helen, we have come a long, hard road. It is not been easy. We have been through the mill and back again. Yet we are still standing and as strong. Our love is always and forever.

My son, Josh who has been something of an inspiration. You have grown into a fine young man. One any father would be proud of. I love you, son.

My daughter, Georgia, in your young life you have had your own struggles to fit in. You have been inspired to carry on. Your strength comes from within, the strongest part of your soul has yet to come. Strive on. You are loved so much. The apple of my eye, and most beautiful girl in the world. I love you, Georgia.

My inspiration from poetry came from many lyricists and I started out as one. Far too many to mention, I know who you are. You are part of my life. A major part of my inspiration. I send out spiritual thanks.

I was drawn back into poetry writing from my formative years by online poetry sites in the early 2000s. The Starlite Café and the sadly missed, Albert. Lovestories (no longer as it was) but a great site of the day. All those amazing undiscovered poets of cyberspace, keep on writing.

Thanks to my soul mentors, our Heavenly Father, Joyce Meyer, TJ Jakes, Kay Redfield Jamison, Joel Osteen, Mike Barratt AKA Shakin' Stevens, Bruce Springsteen, the master Jimi Hendrix, Pearl Jam, Incubus, Elton John, Sade, Aaliyah, Robert Frost, Oscar Wilde, Arthur Rimbaud, Maya Angelou, Friedrich Nietzsche, Frédéric Chopin, Albert Einstein, Christopher Marlowe, Stephen Fry, Will Smith and Sylvia Plath.

My real life mentors, Willie McFaull, Harry Bridges, Arthur Thompson, Cissy MacLeod and Malcom Kerr.

I also aspire to you, the reader, because you come seeking inspiring words to make you smile, lift your spirits, or just to make you think. It might even make you smile or stir emotions you'd rather keep hidden.

In any case, keep on being creative.

Table of Contents

Poet's Notes

Love Hurts
Given To Bleed
The Perfect Lie
Devoted To This Masquerade
As The Heart Waits
Drifting Oblivion
A Wing And A Prayer
Electric Thunder
Watching
Young Girls
Weedy, Seedy Spineless Little Man Syndrome
Write Your Own Eternity
This Withered Life
The Vulnerable War
In My Darkness
Iron Out The Rough Spots
Karma Has Longevity
Love Is Not The Lie
Yes, My Love
Say It Right
This Charming Place
Too Blind To See It
Ode To A Better Man
Tell It To The Man
Through The Darkness
Waking Up In A Minefield
(I Want To Be Like) Stephen Fry
Bellend Barry Of Brodick Bay
Julia
Robin

Disconnected

The Roulette Wheel Is Love

Broken Promises

She's Poison

Blood Of The Innocent

Glencoe

Blood Of My Blood

Love On The Inside

Royally Yours

Unrequited Love's Desolate Heart

Infinite Madness

Grey Days

The Ignominious Deceitful

Breaking Solitude

The Crying Wind

Always Yours…

Bravura Song

Surrender

I Dreamt Somebody Loved Me

The Other Woman

Solitary Man

Rainbirds

Should I Write Her A Poem

The Eyes Have It

A Crushed Disposition Left By Weakness

Timeless

Simply Musing

Painted Lady

Pocketful Of Rain

When That Door Opens

Whiskey In The Guitar

Dream The Dream

Sometimes Like Butterflies

Dreams Are Just The Same

Love Is An Insane Game

Slowly

Why Does A Man Have To Be Strong

Crestfallen

The Day It Rained Forever

Ethereal Love

How Winter Kills

The Acid Well

Father

Tomorrow

POET'S NOTE

I have written over 350 poems in my life, I have enclosed a mere portion for this book. Some of the ones I have written will never be seen in a publication. It takes time to grow as a poet. No matter who says different.

The object of poetry writing is that it flows from the soul. It is a part of you. It means something different to each and every one. I am of the opinion no one should ever explain their poetry. I am of the opinion there is no such thing as a good poet or a bad one. There are simply poems some people won't particularly like. I do think a poet should show themselves to be diverse. Not every poet should simply write, whether there's rhyme or not. I don't think every poem written has to rhyme, but it does have to resemble something poetic. A form, a structure, or a style you can look at with the view of categorising a written stanza into a poem. Then again, who can truly define that? No one I know or have heard of.

Poetry can be as difficult or simplistic as you can imagine. I just think a poet's role, particularly in these times where poetry is not a refined literary class as it once was, is to reach people on some sort of level. Catering to emotions and reading pleasure in as many ways as one can. Poets in the modern world have a more arduous task than our predecessors as we have to strive to make poetry heard, seen and enjoyed. In this age of information technology the written word fights for prominence. It often fails. Poetry is one of these warriors fighting through the mountain of Internet material, console gaming, and easy mobile gadgets including tablets, smartphones, e-readers and so on, to be recognised as a worthy competitor in an education format. Poetry is an education. A lesson of mind, spirit and soul. A lesson of life, love, pain, gain, loss, and creativity.

Can anyone be a poet? Of course they can. You just have to be in touch with your inner being. You must reach beyond the surface. When reading or writing poetry the concept is much the same. To understand what makes a poem, you must first understand the poet, or the poet reader.

I don't ever want to live in a world where poetry is not taken seriously. In the world we live in just now, it is not taken seriously enough. I do hope to build a better future one poem at a time. Poet's side by side, standing shoulder to shoulder with pens at the ready. Poetry rises above any other literature, because these are written about a true person's thoughts, meanders, life, loves and world views. These may well be similar to the reader's. This is what makes poetry unique and endearing to those with a mind to conceptualize its value.

The idea that someone other than myself reads just one of my poems and takes something credible, thought-provoking or inspiring to their lives from it, is amazing to me. It means my job is done. You may not like every written word within these pages, but I hope I capture your imagination. I also hope I allow you to even pick up a pen to allow your muse to inspire some thoughts of your own.

I write often as I feel at that moment, a longing, a thought on the world, a viewpoint of us all in this human race. A lot of my poetry doesn't rhyme, some do. Others take form poetry, which as an exercise I quite like now and then. 'Rhyme Royal' is probably my favourite poetry form, basically because it is so simple and flows so well, and yet within these lines of this particular form you can write so much. Say so much about life, love and the world at large. I also dabble in some other form poetry like the title poem, whose form asks for certain lines to be repeated throughout. Form poetry can be quite fun. But to write, just let your pen flow as you feel.

There is a poet within us all, live it, read it, love it, write it....

LOVE WILL CONQUER ALL

Each of us seeks refuge
From the damage that's been done
Of the evil subterfuge
That our enemies begun
Gracious mercy lift us up
Where love will abound
As each of us develop
Our happiness shall confound

The poor of heart shall perish
Sunk down in the pit they made
Whereas forever we will cherish
The hand true love has played
Those who judged us before
We will put them all to fear
When we blithely ignore
Their attempts to domineer

You will confidently
Put your trust in me
When we shall abundantly
Reap with grace the equity
You cannot forsake the cry
Of two souls who are afflicted
By the hate of those who deny
The malice they inflicted

I will celebrate you
With all of my heart
Fervour will liberate two
Souls who are currently apart
They will sing aloud
Of Eros' wonderful deed
Everlasting and proud
To continue forever in need

We can all play part in the fall
But we know love will conquer all

PICTURESQUE

A blush of sunlight shines
A glistening ray of hope
Multi-coloured
Pious fusion in the sky
Where profane thoughts
Delicately blossom
Like flowers after the rain
Let the spiritual union grow
Secularism
Has no bearing within you
In your subtleness
Sweet spirit you are
A matter of this distrust
Strives to bring disparity
You must live your life
To seek
Valued understanding
To reap
Rewards only you know
Picturesque
In every sense of the word
The gift of you delights this life

ECHOES

When echoes of summer
Fail to reach your mind
And winter's discontent
Is all you will find
In the morbid thoughts
That clutch to the past
When only the memories
Of being the victim
Seem to last
Twisting in the alcove
Of thoughts dead set
On torturing your sickened mind
Until you are so disconnected
From everything – and everyone
Nothing seems to fit
Nothing seems to make sense
Until that one fateful moment
By mere chance
You find –
Love

TAXI DRIVER

These roads were his domain
For so many carefree years
Elegant conversation
A polite smile
As he drove to your destination
One could never hope to meet
A nicer, kinder person on the road
Working away aged seventy-three
He never thought to leave the driving seat
His journeys were inspiring
Intellectual deliberation
Safety consciousness, second to none
You were where you had to be in no time
It seemed like your journey just begun
Always leaving you with appeasement
As we hear his journey has now ended
He died, as he lived, driving these roads
In a taxi to nirvana ascended

BUTTERFLY GIRL

Butterfly girl in flight
With grace and optimism for life
She embraces value from misfortune

Her body is in ruin
Her wingspan is in splendour

Afflictions never bring you down
She flies –

Like a heavenly dove
With faith her strength and guide
To overcome such bane

EVERLONG

I wait
On beaches of golden sands
Staring out to the sea
Knowing somewhere out there
Under these same sun, moon and stars
You may be waiting for me
With aching arms
That hang like tree branches
Weighed down in a rainstorm
With lips – longing
Embracing the wind
Just to feel a sense – a taste
Of the love we once knew
Wasted years; wandering minds
To a place darker than winter night sky
Searching for something
That should always be ours
Somewhere in time; the dark distant past
Becomes a bright, entrusting future
When we find a place to come home to

SEDULITY CANNOT LAST

Misty coloured rainbows
Encased in golden rays of the sun
Peeking through dissipating rainclouds
On a mid-afternoon autumn sky
Where two lovers meet
On lonely street
Walk hand in hand, arm in arm
Living, loving, laughing, enjoying being alive
To see it remain eternally
Or become infernally
Bitter of the virtuousness so fast
When in love
Sedulity cannot last
Mortals fail to attain
In the enchanting affection
Such celebrated perfection
As pleasure seeking hedonists
Who see faultlessness in their mate
As a prerequisite for an impeccable life
To be fastidious in love
Is to bind a heart with an acerbic life
The present becomes the past
Sedulity cannot last
Forever

WHISPERS OF A DREAM

I saw in all perfection
The image of beauty and passion
Where heartbeats echo in the night
Like dreams of children
Are innocent and pure
Visualising a care free world

In all edification
My creative, unquiet mind
Seeks the purity that may dwell
Like a teardrop on a lake
As the river flows
Into the deepest blue ocean's heart

Here in my reality
I hope to make the dream come true
Wishing earth a touch of heaven
The spirits within
Reign fruitfully
To live here together as one

AND THE GODS MADE LOVE

Roving
Through the clouds
In the arms of forgotten angels
Who cry
When we die
Before our time

When I see you smile
Your love smiles on me
Everything is so beautiful
That I see
It's like the heaven's open up above
I see those angels and the gods made love

Teardrops
In a sea
Of timeless fantasy, just because
They define
You're not mine
In my arms

The river that flows
Into oceanic waves
Shows images from above
That saves
When angels send down one single dove
My soul feels you here and the gods made love

Love, whenever we are apart
I still feel, I know you by heart
We fit together like hand in glove
We are found and the gods made love

F.E.A.R

Cross my tainted heart with love
Shine a light into this soul
That is bitter and battered
Forlorn and untrusting
Like a pneumatic drill
Echoing in my mind
Of hopeless indecision
And confusion
Longing for death
Whilst clinging to every breath
Like a child to its mother
When a stranger calls
Held in animated suspension
Above clouds which lead to dark shadows
Across skies of bloodshed soldiers
Who die in a war
On the pretence of defending a country
That has no idea how or why it began
Entrusted with the vision
Of every politician
Who seeks power or revenge
Our lives guided by circumstance
Of the incompetent well-educated morons
Arrogance of men and women
Who leave you feeling forgotten
We buy into this regard
While love left a calling card
Through all our darkness we cannot see
The true meaning of life for you and me
So cry no more tears
Listen to no more fears
False Evidence Appearing Real
We are love
Born *to* love
Lost in love

Close your eyes
Concentrate –
Let yourself –
Feel

THE PLEASURE DOME OF DREAMS

I walk the corridors
Of long forgotten places
I ventured the streets
Of many unknown faces
I met a King
Who stared at me hard and cold
Edward's eyes, many a story told

I mingled at a party
Where *'The Charleston'* music played
I strolled along a road
Cadillac driving teens strayed
I saw the sick
Being tended to by the dutiful young
As the toll of the death bell rung

I climbed a stairway
To heaven where *'The Reaper'* sat
He asked about my life
What had I learned from that
I saw my father
My grandmother and best-friend stood
In all their infinitude

'The Reaper' played a movie
Containing the story of my days
I told him I was not
The kind of spirit who stays
"I'll see you again"
He said, as was my right to know
At the Golden Gate, I rode the rainbow

Descending down the stairway
I saw a child I thought I knew
She told me, *"I'm your past*

A regression of you"
I ran down the stairs
To a life that's real, it seems
Till I visit again, the pleasure dome of dreams

POET'S NOTE

I once had a strange and vivid dream, where I started off in the corridor of my primary school. I saw it as my current self, and was stood directly there in the faculty corridor of that school. I saw the yellow doors and green walls, the windows, playground and football pitch area. The dining room area, the classrooms. The P.E. changing rooms, stairs the lot. The whole experience was so vivid I could reach out and touch the place.

The dream carried on as I turned a certain corridor in the school, I was immediately transported to my Secondary (High) school. Again, so vivid in exact detail. Even certain things about the building and surrounding areas I had forgotten about.

I carried on up the corridor, and unlike the primary school, I could hear classroom noise. To be precise, pupils being taught in these classes.

I ventured to one door. On these doors there were narrow slats of glass just above the handle. I looked through and this class was *my* classroom as I was at around fourteen years old. I was wearing this hideous, shoulder padded, tan coloured leather jacket (It really was very seventies, but I actually loved that jacket).

I could see in that classroom in great detail, my classmates as clear as if they were literally standing in front of me. I tried opening the door, but it wouldn't let me connect to the handle. It was like I was a ghost in this dream and as I tried to grasp the handle, my hand would just go right through it as if I were an ethereal being. At the back of this class was a little girl who didn't fit in there. She was about seven-years-old. She had flowing golden locks of hair and wearing a white flowery dress. She looked directly at me, smiled, and then turned away as if she were listening to the teacher in the classroom.

I was driven in this dream to keep moving. I had to keep going down corridors, or through doors, to reach wherever I was going.

I carried on further up this corridor and as I turned, to what should have been a corridor to further classrooms, I ended up in a dark alley outside. There were no streetlights, it was raining very hard, although in the dream, I was not affected by it. I did not get wet. There was piles of human waste in the streets. There were horse carriages. There was even human faeces in the street. As I crossed over to another dark alleyway. I was met with the same little girl I had just seen in my Secondary School classroom. This time she was wearing rags. She appeared to be tending to a sick adult. I continued to walk up this dark alleyway. In it littered sporadically were more sick people being tended to by children. The sick appeared to be either lepers or had the Black Plague. Also known as the Black Death. I seemed to be in the seventeenth century.

At the end of the alleyway, I turned left through a narrow passage, where a door stood. I entered. I was immediately transported into what seemed to be a palace. I noticed the carpet and recognised a chair, which I saw as Edwardian furniture. In this room, which appeared to be a small study, there were two doors. A set of double doors to my left which were open and looked out into a corridor or hallway. The hallway was not furnished. It was just pure white. The walls. The ceiling. The floor. Everything was a sort of white shiny marble. I could hear voices approach. I then saw a number of men who appeared to be making a fuss of a very important person. He stood wearing some kind of military like dress, which has a yellow sash. He was carrying a helmet.

The man himself was a large, rather heavy man, with a considerable weight problem. His head seemed extremely large. His hair was receding, but swept back over the top of his head. He had a rather prominent moustache and a kind of small beard which sort of made a 'V' shape on his chin. He stopped. Stared directly at me, as if he saw me, and recognised me, but looked as if he knew me but couldn't quite place me, you know that way?

I recognised him as King Edward VII.

His majesty carried on walking, he did not speak or address me in any further way.

To my right was a single door. I knew I had to walk through that door.

I went in, and found myself in a room that seemed to be a party. 'The Charleston' music was playing. As I entered this room, the music stopped and everyone stopped talking to each other, turning directly to me. Strangely, they looked at me for a moment. Then turned to each other and carried on as before.

It was clear from the music and dress of people in this room, I was now in the 1920s.

What the dream doesn't do is give me a reason for any of this.

I pushed my way through the twenties crowd to the other side of the room, where there was a door ostensibly out to a garden area. All I knew was this is where I had to go.

As I approached, near the door, stood a drinks table with waiters stood serving drinks. One of the waiters, dressed in a white tunic, black trousers and wearing white gloves, asked me did I want a drink. He offered me champagne. I drank it. Whilst I could not seem to taste this, I could feel the bubbles tingle in my mouth.

The waiter then thanked me and said I should carry on. He'd see me again. (Unless he was The Grim Reaper later in the dream, I didn't see him again).

I went out into a garden area from the 1920s party. I was on a hilly, grassy area, which I walked down. I could see a road at the bottom of this hill, which had plenty of cars, lights and seemed lively.

I looked behind me. I could see through the French windows (which we didn't have in the 1920s) the party I just left. Above that there was a palace. Further up the hill were my two schools.

I carried on down and arrived at the kerb. I could see many cars, which were dated to the 1950s. I could hear teens in the distance having fun. Lots of laughing and good times. I could hear distant conversation, from which I could deduce American accents.

Across the street from where I stood I saw a familiar Cadillac. It was cream coloured had a spare wheel on the rear side of the car, the tyres had a white rim around them. I said to myself 'hey that's Jimmy's car".

The next thing, there were a familiar bunch of teens, including Jimmy, got into the car. I could name all of them, except one girl who got into the passenger seat aside Jimmy, the driver. It was again one of those I recognise her, but couldn't quite place her moments. As the car pulled out slowly, she looked at me with the same expression.

The car left. I crossed over the road, another driver beeped their horn at me. On the other side of the road, I ended up in a park. It was dark, no lights, all I could see was grass. The only light appeared to be a bright star in the sky. The closer I got, the bigger the star appeared. Until I finally realised this was no star, it was a light that beamed down, eventually coming right down from the sky in front of me. It then materialised into a door.

The door glowed with a white light through the slats. There was nothing attached to this door, no walls, I could literally look behind the door and see more park area.

I opened this door and entered.

I was in a room that was like the corridor where I saw King Edward VII. White marble everywhere. The children I saw in the plague alley were there and came rushing towards me. This time they were all dressed either in white dresses or white suits. The children took my hand and ushered me towards this huge stairway.

The banister was made of gold. The stairway could literally hold ten people standing side by side in its width. I couldn't see the top of it, but I began to climb.

Near the bottom I saw a man, again dressed in an immaculately clean white suit, he appeared to be a 'wino', and appeared quite drunk. He was holding a clear and very clean, empty bottle, which he seemed to be drinking from. Nothing was coming out, but it appeared to him there was.

I carried on up these steps with great pace. Halfway up I could not see the bottom, and still could not see the top. It seemed that I had been climbing these stairs forever. Yet I did not seem affected by the climb. I was not breathless or tired. I continued up, eventually reaching the top.

I arrived on a concrete pathway, to my left and right were two rather tattered looking buildings. Imperfect in every way. Between these and appearing to stand guard was a rather rotund, white haired and bearded man wearing (of all things) a toga.

He acknowledged my arrival with a smile.

Moving towards him were a man and woman who appeared to be dressed in distinguished Victorian dress. He had top hat and tails, she wore a fur shawl, evening dress and carried a delicate, but elegant looking, umbrella. The strangest thing about both, was they appeared to be gliding along, not walking.

The little smiley man in the toga, waved at me and pointed to a door on my left. Encouraging me to go through this door. I did so. As I turned to go into the room, I looked over the rooftop nearby and saw the top of what appeared to be a huge gateway. The most remarkable things about this I saw was the sheer size this gate must be, and how fine a gold it appeared to be made out of.

I would see more of this later.

I entered this room. Again all in white marble. Nothing in the room except a large table and a hooded figure sat with his back to me. This was quite a tall creature. We are talking around two and a half times my height of six foot.

I wandered over and crossed past the hooded figure. He appeared to be moving around figurines on this desktop. Each time he moved a figurine onto a different square this square would light up with what appeared to be moving pictures. Some sort of movie underneath each of these figures, he kept moving from one square to another.

I sat opposite and watched him for a few moments before he spoke. I could not see his face or actually see his hands, the sleeve of his robe seemed to hide them as he kept moving around figurines without even looking up at me.

He asked "What have you learned about your life?"

My answer was I thought life was a joke, some sort of game, in which we were the pawns. I've had a life I didn't want and basically called down every part of my life.

He then asked me "What do you want to do about it?"

As he said that, a door opened to my direct left. Out of which came my father and paternal grandmother. Inside the doorway, smiling at me, was my best-friend. Further inside, I saw my aunt, who is my mother's twin, and my maternal grandmother.

The most significant thing about this? Each of these people were dead. Some for some considerable time.

The first to speak was Willie, my best-friend, who said hello and how good it was to see me again. Willie died almost twelve years earlier to the day I had this dream.

The next to speak was my paternal grandmother. She pointed at me, but addressed the hooded figure, saying "He (meaning me) should not be here. We don't want him here"

To which, I replied "Oh gee, thanks."

My father then quietened her and approached the table. Significantly, my dad, in life, had certain idiosyncrasies. He had a somewhat muffled speech at times, occasionally had a stutter, had a balance problem and was very nasally when he spoke. My mother's twin sister, in life, had a twitch in her left eye and there were certain other imperfections about these people in life. Each of them had none here. Their imperfections were gone. My dad was not what I would call an overly confident man, definitely not the kind of 'take charge' type. He certainly appeared a lot more confident and in full command in this dream.

The hooded figure responded to my grandmother saying it wasn't her choice to be able to send me back as it were.

My dad came forward slammed his fists down on the table and told him in no uncertain terms, to send me back, I shouldn't be here, and I am needed where I am.

The hooded figure did not respond in anyway and continued what he was doing.

My paternal grandmother fired another angry statement at the hooded figure. I was now beginning to think about this whole thing, who the hooded figure was and where I was in the dream.

My dad turned to my grandmother, ushering her and everyone else in the room. At the door of which he stopped, turned to me and said, "It's really good to see you, son, but you don't belong here. Not yet. Go home, son. You should not be here now".

He went into the doorway he appeared from, closing the door behind him, leaving me alone again with the hooded figure, who I now worked out as being "The Reaper".

We sat in silence for a moment with me in a little bit of shock at the realisation of what was going on around me in this dream. I asked The Reaper, "was that my dad and grandmother?"

"What do you think?" He replied, without looking up at me.

I began walking around the room, "I will tell you what I think". I said as I walked, "I go through a series of episodes from my past, and other things I don't understand, I come up a huge staircase, to a room with a hooded figure who produces my dead relatives and friend. I think this place is heaven, you've brought me here, and now we are deciding if I am getting into heaven or not. You are The Grim Reaper. This is heaven" I continued as I sat down again after coming full circle, "Except I am not dead".

At this point The Reaper lifted his head. I could see only one side of his face. He had a sort of gold coloured wart filled face, a huge prominent, pointy nose. His eyes had no iris or pupil. They seemed to be filled with fire. The only one I could see had what appeared to be souls of dead people burning in this fire, crying out in pain.

He raised his hand and pointed his index finger. This was huge, fat, same discoloured texture as his face, with a huge black nail. As he pointed he said "no one said you were",

I briefly saw his teeth, which seemed like huge sharp icicles in his mouth. He was hideous looking.

He began moving around his figurines again and asked "What do you want to do now?"

At which point the entire room lit up like dozens of TV screens on the ceiling, walls and floor were playing episodes of my life. Some of which I remember, some I didn't, until I saw them here. From my birth, to my childhood, my teens, adulthood, my wedding, birth of my kids, everything. It was all here.

Then suddenly all the movies of my life stopped. On the wall to my left was a huge picture of my son, on my right was a huge picture of my daughter and directly in front of me, a movie of my wedding played. The parts of the wedding I remember in my mind the most, were now playing in front of me as a movie.

I got up from my seat and walked towards the approximate area of where the door was that I entered this room. "I'll tell you what I want". I said, confidently. "I am going home"

"Then that is your choice", The Reaper replied. "Are you sure that's what you want to do?"

"Yes, I am sure. Open this door and let me out".

"As you wish". He said, the door opened. Before I managed out, he called out to me. "I will see you again".

"Yeah" I replied, defiantly. "Just don't expect it to be too soon". I left the room and watched the door close behind me.

I was back where I entered. The man in the toga, was still smiling. I walked towards him. His whole expression changed as he became concerned. He put up both his hand in a motion that said 'stop, don't come any further'

"You can't come up here" he said.

I looked beyond him. I saw in all its glory the most amazing sight. The gate I saw a glimpse of earlier. It was shaped like two harps pointing inwards to each other. A huge lock stopped this from opening. The gate was enormous, I couldn't even tell you how big it was, just huge. It was quite possibly the most beautiful thing I've ever seen. It appeared to be the most yellow and purest of gold. Inside each harp shape there appeared to be bars going across it. Each of these bars sparkled in the most unique gems I've ever seen, pearls, diamonds, there seemed to be quite a mixture.

Just through the gate, I could see buildings, paving, roads, grass, trees and cars. These were not too different to houses we have here. Except, everything was impeccable. Pure. So clean. There were no blemishes whatsoever in the building, road or paving. The greenery was the greenest and most flawless you could ever hope to see.

Outside the gate, and next to it, looking almost miniscule next to its vast size, there appeared to be a true to form biblical character. He had a podium and a huge book. Just beyond him was a line of people. Some were families with children, a motorcyclist, and some had been impaled. The man at the podium ushered them towards him. As he spoke to them, he appeared to be writing in the book and taking details from the people in the line.

I looked back at my wee rotund man in the toga. He was never identified in the dream. He was still looking concerned and ushering me back towards the stairwell I originally came up from. I smiled at him and turned back towards the stairs.

I began to descend, looking back at the sights before me. The toga man waved and smiled at me. I smiled back before carrying on down the stairs. I didn't get too far down when I saw the same little girl I saw sporadically at the start of the dream.

She was sat, on a stair, wearing her white dress, this time she wore a crown, which looked as if it had been made out of the petals of flowers. She had plenty more petals, which she threw up in the air over herself.

"Look", she cried out to me, "I'm a little flower princess"

"Yes", I smiled back at her, "You certainly are"

I looked down curiously at her before asking, "Who are you, little girl? Why are you following me around in this dream?"

"What makes you think it is a dream?" She replied, "You know who I am".

"You seem familiar" I said, "But I don't know your name"

"I am you", she replied to me, "I am you before you became you"

I thought about this for a moment, "You are me from a past life?"

"Yes"

"How did you pass?" I asked.

"1936, I was eight. A man in a car", she said cryptically. She continued to play with the flower petals. "You need to go, carry on down the stairs".

I smiled, though not very clear about why she was here, and then carried on down the stairs. Running all the way. When I reached the bottom, the other kids were there from before. Again, they took my hand. Thanking me for coming, telling me they will see me again, but not too soon. They ushered me out the door again at the bottom of the stairs, which should have led me back out to this park I was in before. It didn't.

I found myself in what seemed to be a bar, a public house. It seemed closed, no one appeared to be around. Chairs were on the tables in a fashion that would denote the bar is closed for the night. In the distance, from the light coming in the window from streetlights and the moon, I saw a banner. I could make out the word "welcome". Just as I tried to read all of it, the lights in the bar came on. There was a loud yell of a crowd's "Surprise".

Suddenly, in the room, anyone, who is everyone, in my life was there. All of the 'alive' ones that is. My son, daughter and wife come forward, they handed me a glass of champagne. I began walking further into the room to be with them, as I did, we seemed to fade further and further to black. When it went completely black.

I woke up.

That was my incredible, vivid dream.

I actually have a number of them, this one I will never forget and 'whoa' look out for the book, coming soon!

This dream was the basis for the poem, The Pleasure Dome Of Dreams.

I had this dream at a particularly low point in my life, I was so fed up with everything, and actually longed for death.

This dream came probably as a catharsis. Is there a subliminal message? Is this more than a dream and possibly an out of body spiritual experience?

Well. It certainly poses a number of intriguing questions. Let's just leave it open to interpretation.

LIFT MY SPIRITS HIGH

Kiss me
As only you can do
That sends fire through my body
Embraced in a kiss of joyful lips
That praise the glory of love
That seeks my soul
A dwelling place to rest your heart
A place no one knows
Yet cannot deny
Our spirits rising up on high

Forever be our glory
There'll always be our love
Heaven writes our story
Blessed are we from above

Kiss you
Tender and soft and pure
That takes you to your ecstasy
We proved the battle is won
Inside our hearts
We know the glorification
Of undoubting feelings
Spirit to spirit
Let's make a vow to fulfil it

As we sanctify
Two souls in trust from on high

WINDOWS

I hear, I see you through painted glass
The rain is now gone, let the winter pass
Amour, you are a cluster of flowers
That bloom fragrantly in Eden vineyards
Like a lily growing among the thorns
Your charm weaves comforting kind regards
Rise up my divine one, come away
Deduce, we are favoured with love this day

The voice of the turtledove ripens sweet
Singing of my heart desires discreet
Kiss me with the sweetness of those lips
I turn, as your love tastes better than wine
You are a little rose in summer song
I delight in the fruit that taste so fine
You touched my soul warm within your fire
As my heart enflames burning desire

I come bounding hills and leaping mountains
Cleanse myself in the flow of your fountains
Till shadows flee away and the day breaks
Please hold my heart in highest esteem
I feel my hand as it embraces me
Your voice harmonious as it may seem
Your eyes are like doves elegant in flight
Through the windows to your soul – my delight

THE LAW OF THE LAND

The man who walks the path of iniquity
Who seeks to demean for profitability

The woman who is a scandalmonger and scorns
Whilst living without substance – she warns

Those who prosper in delight and desire
Not to ponder by the flame of the fire

Like a firmly planted tree ready to bring fruit
They will not wither, their values resolute

Unlike the nihilists living without fortitude
To the disrespect and worthlessness they allude

Those who stand justified cannot be bought
The disobedience of the evil comes to nought

The lesson learned is to be in right standing
When fully acquainted with a life so demanding

For in this world what goes around comes around
Each of the execrable in time will be found

The skies are open they will see the genuine
Those living outside virtue will come to ruin

You can never be happy in this life when you
Have intentions to degrade or inflict pain and argue

Whether we like to face up to reality or hide
We all have regulations to live by with pride

EACH AFFLICTED SON

Deliver us from evil, violent men
Who gather together to stir up wars
Their tongues of mischief with poisoned lips
Who kill our children with their sharpened quips
They build a strong foundation
Of total condemnation
Pause and calmly think not once, but twice
Of their desired wickedness, plot and device

These evil men who try to fence us in
May the carnal sin they perpetrate on us
Fall upon them tenfold, Holy Ghost rise
Each cursed tongue unreservedly dies
They do not deserve this earth
And the beauty it is worth
Shelter the integrity of the humble and weak
In your name the principal grateful shall speak

Let malevolence hunt and dethrone each one
Preserve the cause of each afflicted son

ANGEL OF SUBURBIA

She walks these Suburban streets
The world upon her shoulders
No one knows or dares speak of
That which taints her angelic smile

Like the ricochet of a bullet
She hears whispers that echo
Around those walls she builds herself
Skimming the surface of closed in spaces

No one must know as no one shall care
What lies behind her painted smile
It is all locked firmly inside
Hiding the true essence of her being

She works tirelessly long, hard-earned hours
Pretending to all everything is well with her
As her heart enshrines itself, black as coal
Her life is fabricated twenty-four carat gold

Another melancholy song she hears
Deviates to her believing
The fantasy of love, not the reality
She's not ready to face the true picture

She encompasses her thoughts
To a world that seems greener
On the other side, but slowly and painfully
The grass grows under her feet

The vines tie her down in her insecurity
She clings to her cell phone
To send out an SMS of hope
To a trusted or close friend, morning or night

She cries tears of endless frustration
They never dry just merely subside
Until the next downpour of life's creation
Lonely and disturbed as a dream fails

She longs for her amour
To accept her and love her
As she truly is or not at all
Unconditionally

One glass at a time she drowns
Her broken heart like a yelping
Unwanted puppy left out in the cold
Alcohol, at times, her only friend

Yes, the drugs may work for a time
The alcohol soon sobers the next day
The lasting memory of inadequate feelings
Come back again with a bite

She knows whatever is buried alive
Will come back raw and unrelenting
A mere flesh for fantasy on the lips
Of the broken who calls to the night for a prince

She questions her strength
To carry on and be released
From all that haunts her soul
Is there no end to the misery

She's tormented, forlorn and harassed
She finds no solace in the knowledge
There's something better in this world
There's only so much pleading one fragile heart can do

She holds back to convince herself
She is untrustworthy of any good that may come
That she has suffered too much, damaged goods

And could only poison the innocent souls

She reaches far beyond the realms of reality
Encroaching at the door of insanity
Consumed by a mind of morbid thoughts
Anticipation of death a daily occurrence

Until she puts a noose around her neck
A tie knotted to a banister by the stairs
The agony fades as several minutes pass
Only the good die young or are taken

She can see him – she can see him
Although she can feel him she cannot touch
As her spirit dwells within earthly confines
She was far too good for this world

Her amour, her love, such poison that
Sent her way over the edge of reality
Yet, a friend, a possible prince who truly loved her
Longs fervently to be aside the angel who has flown

THE GAME SOLD BY HEAVEN

Like soft petals through an open heart
Leaves rustle in autumn wind and fall
They gently and elegantly glide
As feathered rain cascades a cloudy sky

A leaf drifts till it hits the ground
It is then I wonder, are we drifters
Endlessly flying on angel's wings
Stealing from the King like lovelorn shoplifters

Do we beg, borrow or steal another's tender soul
To use as our freewill dictates the ways
To defile or reconcile by control
To what end? Heartache? Forever? Truth or honour?

I open myself up for more of the same
I could hit the ground with each step I take
Yet, I feel compelled to share that risk
In hope your verity will not be fake

Roll the dice, pray I hit lucky seven
When I play the game we're sold by heaven

PATIENCE

Love endures everything
Illuminating faith to see the best of you
Devotion won't be obsolete
A true gift to make your heart sing
Of an enigma mirroring absolute fulfilment

All the incompleteness, imperfection, crashing
Down thunderously – suitably antiquated
Entrusts pure veracity

Let it be clearly known
We blissfully assured
Can live eternally by our soul's liberty
Although our wisdom may disintegrate
Our love bears up as the greatest of all

A SONG OF LOVE

Are you game fully aware
Or are you duly shy
Passion is in the air
Come under a moonlit sky
Bask in the attention
Natural affection
In splendid advection

We have no need to plan
Let's walk along the beach
There's nothing better than
Talking without the speech
Tall green pines, sandy waves
Where lovers misbehaves
To that in which they're slaves

Spontaneous caress
Imagine where this leads
Not a hint of duress
Implanting both our seeds
Loved ones come onto you
Only as they can do
Set the stage act for two

We feel the water's edge
The waves wash in, so free
As we entwine our pledge
There's nowhere else to be
So tender and so pure
The sea and the allure
Une chanson d'amour

LITTLE MISS BEAUTIFUL

Miss you nights wane this solitary man
Contemplating tender moments alone
Pining tryst, we by love for love, were made
We come with all our hearts and souls do own
We come sharing this love so suitable
I come to you – little miss beautiful

Of broken trust forcibly swept along
We met in dreams of self-inflicted pains
I strained to glimpse you sitting in the sun
True love set us free, bound from inner chains
This through merit, through something dutiful
Encase my heart – little miss beautiful

Love took dull despair making all things new
We were humbled to become best of friends
Keeping faith, meeting failure, or success
We suffered to serve how greatly love intends
To achieve qualities imputable
Those we both share – little miss beautiful

This solitary man will wait once again
Wait, until grace heralds the dawning day
My life to live in your soul's liberty
Fittingly hears my calling, guides my way
Undeterred vision indisputable
Fill me with love – little miss beautiful

THE WEDDING OATH

(RHYME ROYAL)

I owe your love that sealed my heart and mind
There's no price to pay to go deep inside
You have healed me, though I know I was blind
Hand in hand we help each other stay in stride
One on one we walk together side by side
Our Garden of Eden restored everywhere
Spreading love to our children through the air

An act of mercy rode where waters swirled
We said we'd walk together come what may
Angels arm their swords in a fallen world
One last chance to offer a judgement day
In weakness, perfect valour paves the way
A love so strong we can't make it if we run
We have the promise of forever won

Everyone dreams of a love, lasting and true
Sometimes we just see it differently
Should we lose each other, I'll wait for you
Should I move too slow, darling wait for me
Hold on strong whether good or bad times be
So if I should slip free in times ahead
Give me your hand, we are eternally wed

SWEET BIRD OF PARADISE

Over a hazy morning
Flies the bird of Nirvana
A sentient of Edelweiss
Calls without warning
Nature rewinding us
To keep grounding and worthy
Spiritually reminding us
We are not earthly

We wander with graciousness
Streets of material value
We rise to sky view
Of piousness
With wings that spread
In equilibrium
Not a single word said
In the exordium

A measurement of time
Our existence within it
A game played to win it
Of mystical paradigm
Sent here on a heavenly test
So that we may know our home
We should make time to invest
While we're free to roam

When with grace we fly on
Perfectly reincarnated
To be decimated
A new life to pass by on
Paradise forever calling
To fight materialism in life
Freewill keeps on stalling
The fight against earthly strife

When we die, we step into salvation
Into another world
With our essence unfurled
We overview the earth in revelation
Do we become wise
Do we become all knowing
In this place of paradise
Our imperfections are showing

DRIFTING

And if I knew
How it feels to be free
Would it be like
Flying high above
Drifting down the
Lazy river of dreams
Looking at the clear blue sky

All of life's constraints
Held in downtrend rage
Sentiment comes through
Words on a page
A bird of clipped wings
Trying to fly
Through a cloudy, storm ridden sky

An unkind comment
I'm fearful still
Puts me back one step
Taste a bitter pill
The bird tries to sing
Evensong, but you hear nothing
Of my yearning

I'm drifting into stormy seas
I'll come out sometime to a gentle breeze
And the comedic element for you
Will bite back and haunt you to

I'm a caged animal fighting a war
I don't know what I'm fighting for
My hunger years as I drift to sleep
To wake of thoughts so concerning

I can't find strength

To defeat those words
That hurt even now
As I'm dragged backwards
I am drifting still
Through distant blizzards
Looking for the will
To find my freedom

BLACK HEART [BLACK ISLE]

Island of beauty
Visually appealing
Aesthetically pleasing
Harbouring a darkness
A hole – in the soul
Some inhabitants are poisonous
They house a black heart

Words spoken from vicious lips
Of lying toads
Whose heart is as black as coal
Poor little insecure
Contemptuous disparager
Who have already sealed their demise
Time is on the side of the victims
That have suffered their abusive pitch
Karma comes in its own time –
And Karma is a bitch!

UNTIL I'M FOUND

When echoes of summer
Fail to reach your mind
And winter's discontent
Is all you will find
In the morbid thoughts
That clutch to the past
When only the memories
Of being the victim
Seem to last
Twisting in the alcove
Of a mind dead-set
On torturing your sickened mind
Until you feel so disconnected
From everything – and everyone
Nothing seems to fit
Nothing seems to make sense
Until that one fateful moment
By mere chance
You find –
Love

BURNING DESIRE

An ache burns within me
The source of true love
My heart enflames as you are beside me
A carnal desire to feel you
It represents new love
An amazing power to heal you

The beauteous view through love
A prerequisite to durable joy
Love is the key to everything
Hate is the tool to destroy
I yearn successful living
To hold this world in my hands
Free love the stratagem to employ

Compassion from virtue and love
Things humankind has foregone
In life, we often struggle to cope
In search of our Avalon
Desire is a fire that never goes out
Self-belief is a slippery slope
Have faith where there is doubt

Beyond the stronghold of your mind
When crisis takes hold
Wake up to fears falsely unkind
Misrepresenting evidence, you are sold
There's never a better time to be
Taking control for a life refined
No matter what you appear to see
There's no mistaking you are blind
If you accept the bad, but question the good
Yet you wish to be set free
What burns inside helps reaches heights you could
Yet your mind will resolutely disagree

Holding you in contention of your true potential
Where reverence once stood
The desires of your heart are influential
When your fears steal your livelihood

Pleasure and pain conflict, as they should
In the battlefield of your mind, vast and deep
As each day passes, evening becomes morning
The integrity of your soul a mystery to keep
The fire will relight without warning
The hopeful dreams you ache for will be borne
If your desire to believe is strong
When life seems lost and forlorn

POET'S NOTE

Sometimes we get lost in life. We lose all sense of direction. The moment we wake, there is a negative, berating, self-depreciating or senseless thought.

One of the many ways we can seek the joy back in life from those tough days is to take a walk. Just take off somewhere quiet, beautiful and hear the sounds of nature. Smell the scent of the flowers and greenery around you.

Go out into that place. That one place you have where you just want to get away. If you haven't found that place yet, seek it out. When there, just take a walk with nature. Ground yourself by taking slow breaths in and out.

It helps bring back your spiritual self. Helps you appreciate yourself more when you feel out of your depth. Slow breaths, in and out, embracing the nature around you. The sound of the birds, the crickets, the bees buzzing around the pollen infused plants.

Sometimes just getting out amongst the beautiful parts around you is a blessing and joy. It could be a walk in the countryside, a walk to a forestry commission place. If you live in the city, there will be a park near you; a nice beautiful place near a pond, a lake, or just a small lake.

As well as enjoying the sights, the greenery, the plants, the wildlife, you can also seek out flowing water. This may be a small pond in the park, you might be lucky enough to have a fountain or better still, a waterfall.

Embracing the natural elements remind you of your true worth, your beginnings in life and where you are truly from.

Some people in the world today take to trying to dismiss people with curt remarks. Some take to disparaging and attacking. This can start a feeling of lacking in self-confidence. What happens is these remarks or incidents with such people become a challenge to your inner being. You begin to question your worth, accepting that you may deserve their treatment. You most certainly do not.

It's the temperament of the world today. There are so many insecure people around that take to putting others down in any way they can just to make themselves feel better. Remember any attempt of bullying, or just trying to make you look downtrodden in front of others is never about you. It is a true saying it is always about them, and their problems. Hard as it may, lift your head high, and shrug it off. If it becomes abusive to the point you no longer feel safe around them you can remove yourself from that situation and those people, if you can take it to someone in authority, or even a responsible adult unconcerned with it all that you trust. It is always better to share a problem. It goes a long way to help resolve that situation, and stop you being the punch bag for other people's lack of self-worth. It is called "Self" for a reason. It is your responsibility to maintain it. So remove ourselves from situations that bring it down. It is not your responsibility to help others. They have their own battles to face.

Rejoice in knowing it is not about you lift your spirits high.

Do as a dog would do; kick some dirt over that Sh.. and carry on.

One of the best ways is to lose yourself in nature's elements. Life is for living, get your fire back to find a rewarding purpose. It can give you the drive you need to be more assertive in all things.

It's all about self-preservation, my friends.

CLOUDS

I love to lay in bed in the morning
Curtains open, looking up to the summer sky
Watching the clouds go floating by.

I like to make shapes, as they go
A Scottie Dog, a male companion
A cat, bird, dolphin, a dragon

All-in-all it is nice to see
A smile directed back at me

LOVE HURTS

You left me
Desolate, alone and hurt
I ache for you
Despite the fact you cheated
Lied to, and almost broke me
Yet….
…. I still love you so

GIVEN TO BLEED

I *feel* you

Like the morning sun

Like raindrops on my skin

I *need* you

Though you are not here

My breathing is laboured

My mind is confused.

My heart aches constantly

Even though it's abused.

~**~

It's been some years now

Each day is as before

There's never been a let up

I see you in the corner of my mind

Your face, your smile, your hair, your *eyes*

Those *eyes*

I guess you don't get to shake *the one*

The mystery being you are not here

It is preordained before it begun

~**~

The universe, in its wisdom

Tends to treat our emotions

Like a game of Ping-Pong

And when we find eternal happiness

Here on this godforsaken earth

We lose it all

We never get to keep our true soul mate

Listless, in hope, one day we will meet again

Before it's *too* late

~**~

And so I shall bleed *love* bountifully

                The physical pain cuts me off

emotionally

THE PERFECT LIE

Emptiness
On a crowded street
Of torrid indecision
Where you seek to reposition yourself
In search of everlasting glory
In a never-ending story
Of virtuous intent
A voice cries out in the distant shade
Of an imaginary everglade
You hope is heaven sent

Seeking
That to which we're born
For love and by love, it is said
It goes over your head it seems to be
As solitary you stand
Up to love and life's demand
Pursuing what is not real
Until the day this life is over
You lived the perfect lie, you discover
Tell me, how does that feel?

DEVOTED TO THIS MASQUERADE

How do you heal a broken heart
That's muddled and torn apart
That is in freefall
Going bust – to the wall
It crumbles in dissipation
Like hot, dry sand
Through a solemn hand
That never held on tightly enough
Whose fingers let you slip through
Till the sands of time ran out
Leaving me with little doubt
That we were never meant to be
That's what I keep telling myself, you see
At first, I saw no other way
Than to live my melancholy day
Concentrating on one hand
Not seeing what is in the other
Until we reached out for one another
I was not born with one hand, but two
Creating chances
In playful glances
To find love can heal the wound it made
Upon a heart who lived through the charade

AS THE HEART WAITS

One by one the lover's fall
Like ice down a mountainside
From an avalanche
Diamonds on the landscape
Cruising
Decimating
Until it builds back up again
The heart controls a lover's plan
To love, to hurt – at will
To wait, to go
Nobody dies alone
Withering, glowing emblems
Crystalized, carried by the wind
It is not better
To have loved and lost
Where you are
Whatever you do
Out with my control
My heart waits here for you

DRIFTING OBLIVION

The vision of love and its legacy
Lingers like a draw of Marijuana
As it floats around your head hazily
Mellowing your soul, make peace with your heart
Triumphant in finding yourself this way
And I long for the kiss of a maiden
A fantasy to break reality
The world revolved around being "normal"
If this life is what is deemed to be real
I would rather be out there and insane
No one truly likes normal anyway
So why does life have to be so brutal
When all we want is to live and let live
Let us gather our spiritual senses
We can reconnect together as one
If we don't believe in true miracles
Then we don't believe in love's realism
Till its actuality – *drifts away*

A WING AND A PRAYER

Floating
On a bed
Of forgotten angels
Who carry me when I fall
Who barely know me at all
Who bring me to life
Whenever I feel lonely and small

Drifting
On a sea
Of infinite sadness
Who knows me only too well
Got another story to tell
To ruin my life
When those melancholy days befell

Laying
In a grave
That's not yet been dug
Still, it is where I belong
On these days when I'm not strong
Don't want to end my life
Without a fight and battle song

Sometimes
In a daze
I climb your stairway
It's where we meet, right up there
You know my soul is threadbare
You give me back my life
Whenever I fall into despair

ELECTRIC THUNDER

Nightbird flying strongly
In the dead of night above
Lightning crashes
The might of force doesn't wane
Through electric
Thunderous applause

His flight has motive
Thereupon the wash of stars
He clashes with opposition
Composed and untethered
Nightbird flies on

The determination to seek
That which is hard to find
Inspires and compels on cloudless nights
Prolonged days
Singed by electron flow

And he remembers
The cumbersome disaccord
That sets out to hinder
It still cannot stop his flight

WATCHING

I love looking at people
Watching –
From where they can't see me
Every little thing that they do
Each idiosyncrasy
As they walk and talk to themselves
When they think no one is around
The way they dart about the place
Where they hope they can't be found

I observe their very nature
Where it's irrational or can't be explained
Their early morning, laundry on the line, trips
In their nightclothes, when dignity can't be sustained
I wonder what goes through their minds
As they do the silly things, they do
The nameless souls going about their day
Perhaps one of them is you

I love watching people
Who have little common sense
They try to act in all seriousness
When in fact, it's all pretence
I can't help explain
The absurdity I feel
Wherever I'm observing life from afar
I see all people try to conceal

There's nothing more empowering
Than pretending you rule the world
Exposing little secrets
Where vanity is unfurled
As I sit *watching* them go by
Never telling another soul what I see
I often wonder what people think

When they sit alone – *somewhere* – watching me

YOUNG GIRLS

They are beautiful, bright, loving, and kind
Until Friday night rolls around
They start to lose their mind
Alcohol consumption
Begins to fill their toxic lungs
Liver cirrhosis
Before they're thirty-one
They drink in vast quantities
Till they barely remember your name
Every weekend sundown is the same
Live for the end of the week
Like alcohol is their saviour
Girls who drink excessively
Do yourselves a favour
There's more to you than that
Just drinking till you fall
Alcohol is your only fun
Waiting for the weekend to call
Is your life really so degenerate
You need all of Sunday to recover
Your young life wasted
On something you'll pay for later
I suppose you'll see this as preaching
When a lesson is there for teaching

POET'S NOTE

One of the things that really depresses me in his world is the modern need known as binge drinking, especially in young people. You see young lads living it up, acting like total idiots with their mates, but it used to be lesser known in young girls.

I think it is especially disheartening to see young people today live for nothing but the next time they get 'wrecked' as it has been said to me.

Wrecked is exactly what it is.

Sometimes so aggressive because they have a lot of suppressed anger that alcohol brings to the fore. So wrecked they can barely string a coherent sentence together. They have little concern for their own personal safety. Sometimes they can even find it hard to remember their own name.

Why do people drink to excess?

One thing is lack of confidence. However, most of the time it is to forget how their life is and through pure boredom. There is little for teens or even early twentysomethings to do anymore. In many communities, more especially smaller ones, it has all been taken away. We lost community halls, kids and teen clubs, interesting places to meet socially; we are even losing some libraries. Places where young people can promote their creative minds, or at the very least meet their peers on an intellectual level that does not involve the incessant dependency on alcohol.

For all politicians and councils take away from us doesn't seem to cut down our taxes, funny how that works isn't it?

Pure boredom is a beginning but it doesn't end with just young people. All of us are increasingly frustrated with having little to do and being swindled left right and centre by our government of our rights, money and way of life in general.

I recently looked for an afternoon's entertainment in our local area for my fourteen-year-old daughter and some of her friends. There was absolutely nothing on, unless I wished to lay down £45GBP per head to do so.

It wasn't so long ago our son, our nieces and their friends were of that age. My wife and I can remember things on for them almost every day. There were events, clubs or places to take themselves off to, to just hang out. More and more is taken away and barely anything is given back.

These young people, our future generations, deserve more than just living to be drunk. Just to get them through. There is nothing wrong whatsoever with having the odd night out which involves getting a little drunk, or even a good bit drunk now and then, but when it is a regular occurrence and you can hardly wait to be drunk again it isn't any kind of true existence at all. Just drinking to escape the mundaneness is a failing on us all as a society.

Rightfully, in that respect, blame lays firmly with politicians and councils who take it upon themselves to deprave people with the right kind of creative outlets or social pleasures that don't necessarily involve alcohol is simply unjust and entirely wrong. All for the so-called budget cuts, that affect everybody else except those actually making them. The fat cats and the expense account elite that pocket the difference, putting little use of funds back into communities. When are we all going to wake up and realise the whole affair is corrupt and we let them get away with it, because we do not stand up and say, "no more".

We're being robbed of our lives and hard-earned cash to help the greedy, not the needy.

What's more the increase in binge drinking will have a knock on effect down the line, when in twenty years all those drinking to excess results in more sick days and a strain on health services through illness.

I really do despair when I see how the young people act in society. The answer according to politicians is to put a hefty price tag with minimum pricing per unit for alcohol. The answer is to stop taking our frigging money, lives and rights and give more to people and for people to do with their lives.

There's little to do nowadays that doesn't involve having a good time by getting *on it*. People don't know anymore how to have fun unless it involves getting drunk. How pathetic an existence we've let ourselves be led into. Social networks are full of young people writing with glee just how drunk they are going to get, miserable before, happy at the thought of just getting completely and utter wrecked on alcohol.

I hate to see this world fifty years from now, I won't be around, but that's not the point, we should all be concerned with preserving long-life, looking after the planet, and safeguarding a more intelligent future than the majority of fun-times being laced with alcohol. We have great difficulty preserving anything when the only sense of freedom or enjoyment is lost to being drunk at any given chance.

It is so sad we in the world with likeminded people sit and take this political term after political term.

The solution is to bring back community spirit. Bring back something to give people the desire to live again. The fire inside, the fighting spirit to do something more fulfilling, mature, intelligent and rewarding in the long term. Have a good night out, but not live for those drunken escapades as the highlights of living. People need to be given the tools to work towards successful living.

As for the more political problems we face, I think it was British PM Margaret Thatcher who said something along the lines of no one should be Prime Minister (UK) until they have a great deal of experience. What she means is moulded into the way we do things in British politics. The same can be said of any other country, I think. What really needs to happen is we take everything we know about how politics are in this country and dispose of the lot of it. Start again, and move towards helping the people find successful ways to make a long-standing living and truly keep the economy afloat. This means stopping the political views of helping the rich get richer, catering to big business and the banking system and putting that money in the hands of the people who make the economy work. The average people, the worker on the street, the person who lines all these corrupt individuals to safeguard our welfare system and banking systems when all they've done for decades is rob us, defraud the system and work it for themselves. Let's not think the expenses scandal in British politics is something new, it's been going on since its inception.

Each newly appointed leader or elected government let us down, term after term. Let our young people down and then all they do to forget or defeat the boredom, turn to alcohol and so we come full circle. A perpetual cycle no one seems keen to stop anytime soon.

So sad an existence and yet we do nothing to prevent it.

Wake up and stand together as one. Not one person can change the world, but the collective

voices of a nation, each nation, together, truly can.

Be a part of that change. Each country. Together as one. We all want to change the world.

WEEDY SEEDY SPINELESS LITTLE MAN SYNDROME

He is a little man
Bald on top
Hair on the sides
Seedy
Weedy
Altogether needy
Backbone challenged
Heart of a mouse
Shockingly sleazy
A hopeless little nobody
Who conforms to others
Like a moth to a flame
A useless prat
There is *no* end to that
Therefore, would it totally surprise you?
To find they made him Manager
I thought he has something
Over the CEO
It's the only way, you know
Because he could barely
Manage to have a sh… Oops!
I thought I heard him coming
Maybe not, still I find it quite appealing
I'm not really sure why
The spineless weedy, seedy little man
His name will rhyme with 'lie'

WRITE YOUR OWN ETERNITY

For certain people their fate is seen
Those who contradict the grace
And morality of life

The dreamers who are corrupt
Abusing their position
To deny the rectitude

They revile, scorn upon
Slander and reject with abrasive condemnation
The glorious ones, with honour

Reject everything that they do not
Happen to be acquainted with
Irrationality and contemptible

Whatever they do not understand
Or cannot appear to pollute
They annihilate in dissidence

Clouds without water swept along
By the winds of evil and gloom
In eternal misery and darkness

They convict the impious in their judgement
As now and forever, it is written in
The acts of their eternity

THIS WITHERED LIFE

Pocketful's of dust
Fill the air with putrescent embers
Of trees partially sunk in spring waters
A secluded, somewhere of beauty
That belies a place you'd choose to die
Birdsong echoes periodically through the air
That has no words or makes any sense
At least to us
The greenery decays
Unkempt and mangled
Lost, disconnected from this world
Such as I – such as you
No one knows the truth
Or answer why we exist
In a world filled with condemnation
Spitefulness and hurt designed
To tangle your emotions
Like the trees and the grass around me
Corroded – dying
As you on the inside
And yet look
Despite its tarnishing
There is still splendour to be had
All around

THE VULNERABLE WAR

I hear echoes
Of continuity
That revere even the finest soul
Where a heart lies bleeding
Where a mind is conceding
To the bitter after effect of poisoned words
That come from mouths who cross a line
Between love and hate
Excruciation and condemnation
That which is spoken
From lips of lethal weapons
That wound a tortured spirit
Often beyond repair –
Those who enjoy the power
Of inflicting their battle plan
Lonely, damaged, people
Who must choose disparagement on others
To push away their own insecurities
When all you're left with is asking what
What is it all for? –
No one can win the vulnerable war

IN MY DARKNESS

In my darkness, I feel bereft
An empty soul with nothing left
A cloudy day that never clears
A tortured soul with endless fears

I am on this road going one way
No fuel left to come home some day
Travelling an infinite track
Through eternal tunnels, no way back

I'm a steam train on a mission
Roll through my mind of suspicion
Nothing left to feel, but alone
Leaving pain cutting through heart and bone

The torment plays forevermore
Like an addict waiting to score
Losing all sense of who I was
To something irrational, just because

In my darkness, there is no light
I seek solace each day, each night
A mind controlled at every take
By a disease designed to break

POET'S NOTE

Even today, there is still a stigma around depression. As soon as you mention the word people start to distance themselves, probably feels like they judge you too. They seem to often decide you're a danger, because to them only people with depression are reckless or at risk of attacking you.

Other people have the perception you are best left alone. Therefore, they ignore or move away from you. Someone with this disease, and let us get that straight here and now it is a disease, needs some support. A simple kindness can mean a lot.

Many people in this world need to educate themselves about the condition. Depression does not mean you are dealing with someone unstable to the point of violence. Ridiculous and offensive!

One in four people have some form of depression. It can be a mild case. It can be severe. It can be determined to be Bipolar Disorder. I absolutely despise that phrase. I think it should be discontinued immediately from use. It is an insult. The condition used to be known as Melancholia. This is certainly a more mature way of looking at it. It is exactly how a person suffering from depressive episodes feels the majority of the time.

A close friend of mine spoke to me about a mutual friend who had been recently diagnosed. She gave a short laugh when discussing it.

"We all feel a little down at times, but you just shake it off and carry on," she found it laughable.

If this is your view of depression, you really need to shut your mouth because you have no idea what you are talking about whatsoever. Most depressions are not something you simply 'shake off'. It is juvenile and degrading to think like that. Perhaps if you treat someone with depression like that, YOU are part of the problem.

Imagine wakening each morning to negative thoughts, often around the theme of death, suicide or dying. It can be hard to remove these thoughts throughout the day. You are disconnected from the world. Nothing feels real. The trees, the cars, the people, anything, and everything seems foreign to you. You feel like you don't belong. You are in the wrong place. This world is not your world. It all seems alien. You feel no one is around or cares for you, or will miss you, if you die. You feel so alone in everything.

Can you imagine the implications of being so disconnected from absolutely everything and almost everyone around you? How would that feel?

You can't really imagine anything of the sort unless you are going through it. Perhaps, if you feel a strong empathy with someone who is, you might have some idea, but not totally. You are always questioning yourself and your abilities. Constantly berating yourself with thoughts of feeling useless, as if you can never do anything right.

Those tormented thoughts of self-depreciation, dying and generally feeling you don't belong, go on every day. For some, very few hours of each day are without fear or thoughts of this nature. You get anxious about everything. People looking at you, you think are judging you. When you see people walk on by your house, you feel they can see you, peering in through the windows of your house at you. It feels like the walls are closing in. you feel you can't associate with people, lack of self-esteem tells you you're not worthy of their time or love.

You can have everything possible; money, possessions, a loving family, a good career even, but still these morbid, disturbing thoughts constantly haunt you.

This is why depressives look to suicide. They feel it is the only way to escape the fears and irrational thinking. Suicide though is a permanent resolve to temporary situations. Bad times cannot last if you seek the apropos help.

If *you* or anyone you know is feeling this way, take yourself to your doctor. I won't make it sound like a miracle cure awaits you, but there are many options to help you manage your depression and live a meaningful life.

Reach out to somebody today.

You *can* get better with help. I know the idea of talking to your doctor is a scary prospect for someone with depression, but even if they have to be taken kicking and screaming, they will think it was the best thing they could do. The very nature of the disease tells you 'it's OK', 'We don't need doctors', 'You will be fine'.

If you are struggling, or have difficulty functioning to do even the simplest of tasks, or have any thoughts detailed here, or similar ones, you should not suffer alone. There are many resources out there to help. There are many for family members of depression sufferers also, as you also often need help and support to cope.

If your partner or relative or friend changes. If they become argumentative to the point of aggression, these anger issues could be part of the onset of something else.

These thoughts can pass; you may only need some form of medication for short periods. This can help you think more clearly and see things from a positive perspective. All you have to think about is maintaining successful living, and a functioning existence in this world.

You may need to find some passion for life again. You have lost your fight. The fire that needs to keep on burning to help you through life, it must be allowed to breathe, and keep stoked or it can die.

Find something you're good at. Something worthwhile and rewarding – depression=lack of purpose.

A purpose for your life is out there. If you can find something that can help you feel proud of yourself for once, something that gives your life back that feeling of being needed or wanted.

I almost certainly guarantee you are a very creative person. Find your creative zest to help yourself and begin to enjoy life.

Sometimes you do have to confront that which you are afraid of, worries and fears. What has worrying ever done for you? Nothing but steal your joy. Fears and worries are plaques of the mind that serve to sway you from your true path. Think of these worries or fears, circumstances in your life that say to you 'I worried myself almost to death over that'. I guarantee the morbid thoughts that led to fear and worry were never half as bad as your mind allowed you to think they were.

Depression is temporary at least in the sense of stopping you living. Emerge from the dark, get into the light, and make life worth living.

I believe in that. Now you can to. You *can* do it.

Always know you are loved no matter what you think, and by whom may even surprise you if you look, the nature of the disease makes you think no one is there. I am. I tell you, DJ loves you and there is not a damn thing you can do about it.

Be blessed. Please seek out someone to help, it is worth it, I promise you.

No life should be lived in confusion. There is always a way out to give you something to live for. Choose life. Enjoy it and be free.

IRON OUT THE ROUGH SPOTS

Perhaps life's difficulties
Are more imagined
And feared
What I mean to say is
A situation is only made arduous
If we confront it
With pessimism
Lack of farsightedness
Our own downtrodden
View of looking at things
Allows only for torture
Which only appears real
When in fact
All we have to do is open our mind
Be more amenable
And push our hopelessness
To one side
We all have our battles
Tormented thoughts to deal with
But we can smooth over these
By unlocking the stronghold
Of false imaginings
From a contemptuous mindset
Locked in only to hinder
Rather than help
Through the roughest of ties
Optimistic fortune
Isn't hard to find

KARMA HAS LONGEVITY

Being weak as I am
Brings scorn and contempt
Lies – from the lips of those
Weaker than I
Whose testimony belies the facts
That no one is prepared to see
You corrupt me
Destroy me
With the derision that gives you power
Brings favouritism in the eyes and minds
Of those with less intelligence
Than a zombified flesh eating corpse
Contentious naysayers
Who are as belligerent
As they are witless
They speak from ill-advised tongues
To spread injudicious stories
As long as you and I know the truth
Karma will do the rest
Even if it takes a decade or two at best

LOVE IS NOT THE LIE

Love is never meaningless
When you feel all that it can do
The joyful or turbulent emotions
Of what loved ones put you through
Love is never senseless
When you cry inside for what is lost
If torrid sentiment encapsulates
Every part of your body at any cost
Yet there's always hope for love renewed
To bring joy when you're subdued

Let joyfulness adorn
Still we always question the good
We push away and lose our precious thing
Accepting the bad as if we should
And at each breaking dawn
We wake to see another day
To find we never know who we are now
Instead of finding joy in the words they say
Why feed fuel to this burning feud
Believe love is misunderstood

So if you're cheated, lied to or cursed by
Distrust the person, for love is not the lie

YES, MY LOVE

Yes, my love I arouse
Looking for your caring smile
A kiss of tender lips
A hug in the morning sun
I've been waiting all the while
You the light I always knew

No material possessions
Or monetary profusion
Have blessed this homespun
Life, through its trials and confusion
We've remained devoted
Our hearts and souls in reclusion

Though you are so far away
At times, when I need you to hold
Each day that passes fills my life
With fondness still prevailing
Treasured until we meet to
Waken side by side

SAY IT RIGHT

Blessed are those who find joy in their heart
To trust one another as we were intended
Blessed are those who share their life
With someone precious and endearing
All the while believing
In the love everlasting
They carry with them day by day

Faith held are the true soulful emotions
That bring peace and joy to make you feel contented
Hope-filled are those who share these things
With every one they happen to
And just these thoughts make it true
So turn your mind, believe I say

I feel it's time you confessed
Say it right and bright 'I am blessed'

THIS CHARMING PLACE

There's something wrong in paradise
Scandal their weaponry
Can't contain their tittle-tattle vice
Spoiling sanctuary
Heaven cones with an excessive price
Glorious scenery

The beauty is emancipated
If you will volunteer
As the victim anticipated
By sourness of fear
Their self-doubt is extirpated
In the splendour filched from here

How this picturesque scene will cripple
If we allow control
Subdued convictions without scruple
By the grace that they stole
This charming place houses ugly people
With tongues that shame their soul

TOO BLIND TO SEE IT

O Sweet mystery of love so bold
Where are you now, for I've been told
That you are easy enough to find
That you are close to me
But I am blind
I cannot see
O mellow heart of love so fair
When do you come
And start to care
Where is this fortune I've been told
Is worth waiting on
And its weight in gold
For fortune and fame
Never drew me in
But being alone
Is that a sin
O to share this heart
With one so true
One who's always there
One that is you
I just open my eyes
To see through this disguise
To find you in the place I'm at
Beside me all this time
Well, now how about that!

ODE TO A BETTER MAN

If I did not fail you
To provide the pleasures and comforts too
With teachings of life as you grow
And love as you may know
Would strengthen you so
My protection made your confidence shine through

If I were a stronger man
A hero with an almighty plan
To secure your trust in life
Whether you be a husband or a wife
You'd have the tools to cope with strife
To reach beyond the mundane to be all you can

Had I served you well
As I sit here and dwell
On all the things I could have done
Whether you be my daughter or my son
But of me there's only one
There's a path to life I cannot tell

I may not have brought riches
My deluded plans may hit glitches
But if I have taught you one thing
It's to be true to yourself and bring
The joys you find; the songs you sing
Over and above trouble's little itches

TELL IT TO THE MAN

Weakened by the honour
Of the segregated hand
Of love, kindness, manners, peace
All of which elude this land
I am embittered and torn
Into this life I've been sworn
I did not see it coming
I did not make this arrangement
To be in solitary containment

Has each of us forgotten?
Where lies the boon of our souls
Where community spirit
Gave us prestigious goals
There is no understanding
Just egotist demanding
No one is as friendly, or
As kind or decent as before
We're building walls; locking the door

The world cannot see us
People understand nothing
Of anyone anymore
Still we must stand for something
Or anything makes us fall
When the reaper comes to call
You haven't accomplished the plan
Have an excuse; go tell it to the man

THROUGH THE DARKNESS

Broken soul, a vagrant of lonely street
Adrift – disorientated – condemned
Feels forgotten, untrusting, incomplete
Barely knowing from where the darkness stemmed
No one dares to speak a kind word or two
Lost in a world that clearly doesn't see
Until I found a difference in you
Someone who is devoted to me

Melancholy, disenchanted with hopes
That cling to a morbid past, you bring light
To the darkened tunnel where this soul copes
With looking death in the eye day and night
Covered in love as leaves on autumn ground
Soft rose petals, a delicate flower
In a mind where silence cannot be found

You feel you never know quite what to say
Yet, those few loving words are all I need
I would never be who I am today
Without the power, you bring to succeed
We've been through hardships, breakups, tears galore
Those times brought faith and strength to see we will
Be as one, we never needed this more
You're aware I may stumble, as I'm still
Climbing mountains to be more than I was
We shall fight, the blackness we will smother
We will reach journey's end simply because
We both have each other

WAKING UP IN A MINEFIELD

There is only a sense of doubt
As the morning migraine takes hold
Waking up with blinding pain
Across the head; behind the eyes
That sickly feeling; the inability to function
By no means an ordinary headache
That can simply be shaken off
Debilitating or explosive

The first flicker of an eyelid
The first taste of an excruciating ache
Close your eyes; resort to a dark place
Light causes the sting to hit
Like the rapid fire of a soldier's gun
Until you feel as if you're in a minefield
One wrong move to a painful explosion
Going off where you're left enervated
Until a moment of clarity
You are freely out of the danger zone

BANG!!! another rocket flares fusion in the sky
Not like a pretty rainbow or firework display
A rippled effect in your head causing a stir
In the pain receptors of your mind
An echo as if through a large alleyway
To loud and thunderous applause
Like a hurricane whirling, twisting and destructive
It may settle down, but never dies outright

(I WANT TO BE LIKE) STEPHEN FRY

I see him through the media
I don't know him outside in
Stephen, doesn't know he encourages
He'd say, 'I wouldn't know where to begin'
His life brings meaning
To all who follow his ways
I meet life with a boredom sigh
I want to be more like Stephen Fry

Weakened by emotion
Causing the commotion
Lamenting notion
Shining through devotion

He won't pretend he's a strong man
Though he will eloquently say
What he thinks of the condition
That makes him feel this morose way
Melancholic and dejected
He helps us all to understand
The ink flows – I let my pen fly
To this inspirational guy

He will peek inside his lost soul
Even if it feels sad or cold
He believes in fighting and standing tall
As darkness has him in a stronghold
Not afraid to talk about himself
He'll stand for what he believes in
I want to be like Stephen Fry
Who's all about *do* or *die*

BELLEND BARRY OF BRODICK BAY

Now, Barry is a sturdy man; conscientiously fat
His wife has him on a diet, but he's having none of that
When she's not around to feed him *granola*
He'll have two bacon rolls instead
It seems his portly belly is never truly fed

Now, Barry is a snide man, who lives in Brodick Bay
It's a shame he's not as charming, as he sometimes will portray
He has a 'thing' for a co-worker
Hoping for an affair?
One wonders why they don't get a room together
Their spouses blissfully unaware

Integrity, honesty and wholesomeness
These things with Barry, the Lord did not bless
Raging hormones have him act out and smite
In all his eighteen stone and medium-average height
So pathetic a man
Full of pettiness and spite
Through his overbearing insecurity
To appease her uteromania
And to feel better about his poor self, you see

Now, Barry is a bellend, his head shaped like a penis if you must know
If he fancies being a real man, I'll honour it if he wants to have a go
But Barry can only act through this corrupt mind
Which makes him a proper bellend, I think you will find
So sad the sound
So frightful the sight
He hides behind his shifty smile
His irksome maliciousness
Is just his cowardly style

Barry tries to be proud but walks at an awkward pace
Chewing gum rapidly when he's not stuffing his face

His belly-popping shirt, hanging woefully over his belt
Hoping not to break wind, and its aloof wetness to be felt
So sad the sound
So torrid the sight
Of a man dejectedly repressed
Barry's vindictiveness did not work
He must feel sick to his irritable bowel, when he sees how I've progressed

JULIA

Julia and I had an affair
When her husband wasn't there
We made love on the bedroom floor
Not once, but twice and one time more
She said her husband 'ignored' her
I later found the poor man adored her
We'd talk in secret and plan forever
Which she had no intention of fulfilling ever
We did not convort on the marital bed
I should have realised what lay ahead
I was not her only, there were a few
Randy, Marvin and Joey too
She was the puppet master who did the toying
Destruction of lives she seemed to be enjoying
She telephoned Joey's wife out of hate
She told her of the affair to put her straight
I took a chance throwing my heart on the line
What if she's telling the truth but what if questioning is a sign
Nothing answered, an if, or a but
And what you get for falling for a slut
I pity her poor husband, I must confess
When he finds out about her mess
Julia and I have parted ways
Some other fool falls for her lies these days
The innocent in these situations pays

~**~

You can't help who you fall in love with, but you can help lying and hurting the other people not involved. If things are not working out, or you are unhappy, and you meet someone else whilst married or in a relationship, finish one and decide who you want to be with. Cheating and lying gets nowhere, but a whole world of hurt.

ROBIN

Melodrama; funny man; gone too soon by his own hand
Loved so much, it's hard to understand
Why he didn't want to stay
Why he's not here today
Lost and alone even in a crowd
Unable to control the incessant malady
All it wants to do is get you alone
In a room to kill you
It seems the only way out
Depressive episodes leave little doubt
The legacy of Robin is clear as day
Even though he had his critics
Some say, he was overly sentimental
Still he reached out to someone, sometime
O how I loved him throughout my life
His smiling face, a funny quip, a loving embrace
He helped so many, through thick and thin
Yet no one seemed to be there for him
If only I had that opportunity
If only I could have been nearby
I could have seen he didn't die
If one thing has come out of this today
It's for us all to look after ourselves in every way
So funny man here is your valediction
I pray your time on earth is remembered well
And the rest of us who are cast with the infliction
This terrible disease we can only hope to repel

DISCONNECTED

When everything feels alien
I'm bored by my surroundings
The people you care about
The things you loved to do
Only feels like an emptiness to you
Where there is light, darkness falls
I feel like an empty waste
As if I have no real form
I am faced with blackness
Of the very, great deep
When did I last sleep?

My body feels like I am here
But my spirit moves in different circles
The light cannot be separated in nyctalopia
There is no rule over day or night
I have only blindness as my sight
The water hasn't separated from the sky
No earth – no seas – no vegetation – no trees
The expansive sky shines no light on my land
No birds fly in the open of heaven
Life bears no fruit; no more go forth and multiply
There is only an existence called 'Living To Die'

I see everything on Earth that's been made
I hear the songs oftentimes played
Yet cannot connect to any of it
In my home, my life, my love, my country
There is only strangeness I am seeing
O give me breath, the spirit of life
So I can share this world a living being

THE ROULETTE WHEEL IS LOVE

Falling in and out of love with you
Seems to be the done thing in all of my days
Thoughts gather like volcanic eruption
Then wither down in the dying ash
You spin the wheel; roll the ball round and around
Throw your chips in and take your chance
I know I've thrown my heart on the craps table
Far too many times on a lonely night
There has been the days of hurt and tears
Hope then despair, wondering profusely
Where our foray into amoré will end
We have no future toying around
Heartfelt words feel more like
Holding onto your last chip of hope
Nothing ever feels the same
No matter what you have or who
When you lose the one you love
Despite the hardship, frustration and pain
You'd give that last golden chip to the dealer
Just to spin the wheel one more time
In hope of having them back again to stay
Somehow you go on, listless of the soul
A brave face, a fake smile
Still, nothing brings back that feeling
You can only hope they're happy now
Even though you still feel painful memories
That seems to corrupt and enflame
Until the next casino and yet another game

BROKEN PROMISES

They drift along the courteous soul
Like a cloud weaving through the darkness
Echoing from the depths of an endless cave
Of forgetfulness and grimness
They sear at the heart of the afflicted
The tongues of the conflicted
Trysts unfilled have no way
Of moving forward
Misty coloured mornings
Haze over the mind of forgotten angels
With good intentions
Excuses for desertion
Become inventions
Never ever executed –
Effectively
Each step taken is always backwards
A forlorn and unappreciated feeling
Roars inside those on the receiving end
Of gaucheness

SHE'S POISON

She's poison
Venom fills her evil heart
It is as black as the coal
That fills my fire
She burns people with no care
She makes no distinction
Between decent friends or enemies
She roams this little island
Like butter wouldn't melt in her mouth
But she *IS* poison –
Of that there is no doubt

Her peroxide hair
Speckled with grey
An embittered smile
To make people feel safe
So that they warm to her
Like the friend you long her to be
Just like the snake that she is
She lays in wait to encircle her prey
Like a mantis waiting to strike
O yes, she's poison
Watch her venom come on out

The vulgarity of her species
Lurking indiscriminately
Her pounding heart
Black as the ace of spades
Preying on the weak and vulnerable
She's a juggernaut
Hammering home her hate
To dissociative souls
She doesn't care who the victim is
That woman is poisonous
A vileness that flows with no drought

BLOOD OF THE INNOCENT

Blood of the innocent
Spills in wars of power gods
Where no one honours the gift of human life

False gods who flow poison through their veins
Care nothing for the innocent

Eyes that seek death from afar
That see no blood shed on poor streets

Belligerents who cause the depraved
To live meagre lives of panic

Their tongues spawn orders of blitzkrieg
Hostile to the weak
Let them beg on their knees in fear

GLENCOE

Many of my ancestors died
In a Scottish Highlands battle
A mêlée that should never be
In history
A glorious revolution
It's said where a King is dethroned

Forty women and
Children needlessly die of exposure
As their homes were burned
In allegiance to the next King
The Jacobite uprising took an oath
The Captain in command
Send one hundred and twenty men
To massacre those who would not fight

The snowy hills
Ultimately becomes the grave
The clan MacDonald wiped out in shame
O Captain Hill your demons rise
As you took them all by surprise
Your men climb the Devil's Staircase
Heinous
Criminal; four hundred men
Went up the hill from Kinlochleven
What was Colin Campbell's part?
Across the waters
Of Loch Fyne to break the clan
Thieves in the Valley of Glencoe
Did you find a willing accomplice
In others who bore the Campbell name?

The MacDonald clan fled
Killed in their bed in gutless style
Secure all avenues

Let no man escape

The Rebels
The MacDonald's of Glencoe are called
The order came; put all to the sword
There should be no feud or favour
At five O' clock; plan to action
It's all for King and country
Slaughter, defile; degrade
Nothing has changed
We, still massacred by the hand
That rules over us for Queen and country
The battle goes on

Unceremoniously a pardon
Granted for those uprising
In allegiance to a King anew
Reprisals to all who do not conform
It seems to me nothing has changed at all
We are still the Clansmen
Massacred daily by the government and throne
Slaughtered emotionally each time
We look at our pay
Or watch TV
We never even took that oath

Like Duncan Rankin shot down
Miscreants cut off at the root
We die each day to pay our way
Whom do we apportion blame
For the centuries of a war torn heart
Yet we romanticise life
In allowing the persecution
To go unnoticed like Glencoe
So how long will they mourn us?
Weeping at our memorial
The Clansmen of heart

To the
Massacre of Glencoe

BLOOD OF MY BLOOD

O blood of my blood
Make what you can
Of this intolerable land
Do not give rise to fear
Such as I
Who beset his life
From year to year
Encouraged by yielding
To the thoughts of failure
Which held him back utterly
Stopping him being a man
Make what you can
Of your talents and creativity
Be all you can be
Remember all we taught you
-    Your parents
To have the confidence we didn't
O blood of my blood
Do all you can do
To help others less fortunate than you
You are pure and forthright
Shine on – shine bright

LOVE ON THE INSIDE

As the cock crows
The lily grows
In fervent beauty
Around the garden of hope
In sun shone greenery
It inspires a closeness to nature
As the morning birds sing
Their songs of contentment
You watch them eat their seed
So far removed from paradise
In the scorn and poison
That surrounds this earth
Prompted to reminisce of His intention
When He created this invention
That splendour that envelops us
We neglect to see each day
Reminds us morning light is a blessing
Where a little piece of heaven
Can be found as we live
So we journey on
Peace within grows if we forgive
This love will bring a brand new dawn

ROYALLY YOURS

I love you because you hear me
My soul has a plan
Only your heart can understand
There will be no one unless there is you
I intend to be exclusively true
You can call me yours as long as I live
As long as my heart beats it has love to give

I have suffered anguish and sorrow
Until you saved and delivered me
You give care plentifully
You bring me life; you dry my tears
When I stumble and fall, be the one who steers
This world is full of deceitfulness and lies
You bring me a new day with clear blue skies

I believe in, trust, and cling to your love
I walk in your land of giving
You give me a voice in my conflictions
I will lift you up; I will call your name
I will take these vows and never be the same
Precious is the light that shines down
When abreast of you, I wear the crown

UNREQUITED LOVE'S DESOLATE HEART

We sat by the river
Tears hallmarked two hearts
Trees rustled in the wind, the birds sang
As here the goodbye starts

Finally letting go
And if forget you
Let my penmanship lose its skill
For words written untrue

You who led me captive
Release me in birdsong
Yet as I walk in a strange land
My torment you prolong

As love requited
This was never your dream
Like Babylon my heart will fall
And shatter as I scream

No matter how it plays a desolate part
Your words spoken served you well and
Claimed my heart

INFINITE MADNESS

There are echoes going further
Than the realms of one's own mind
Voices carry like lances in the night
Startling me awake
As they call my name
Demonic faces growl at me
From darkened corners in the wilderness
An infinite madness soaks my body
Like a constant flow from hell's waterfall
Of flames, burning bright orange and red
Where does the insanity end
That beseeches me from afar
Lost to me
Is the soul with which I am borne
Despite the angels
Sending me their comfort
A robin looks out
From the branch of a tree
Staring deep eyed at me
A memory
A motion
A tryst of heaven
A message to me
Of deliverance from evil
From this evil-minded game
Where Lucifer tries to claim
The true heart of a lost soul, lonely
Desperate, searching for a road
To where the sign points the way
Still, I see no sight of this sign today

GREY DAYS

Where has my innocence gone
The naïve young me
Lost in a sea of bitterness and anger
Disparaged by the people
I sought to seek well of
Who left me drowning in such a sea

I sought the good, blind to the bad
I hoped overall for a better place
A world where love ranges
From brother to sister to everyone
Who will be together as one
Where the sun shines on their face

I once saw beauty everywhere I went
The colour of the world was blue
Until the wicked hearts and minds
Of those whose only pleasure
Is to end the happy nature of others
Destroyed my hope to make grey days true

Mystery surrounds the way of the world
As to why we're loaded with hateful
Malevolent creatures lost in a decay
Of blackened souls putrid in their own dermis
You can smell the burning, rotting flesh
Of those eternally ungrateful

I hate the world today the people
Who make it hard to want to live
Those who steal your joy and zest
Whose day of reckoning doesn't come soon enough
They say clemency is good for the soul
Those transgressors make it hard to want to forgive
We can only hope for Angels calling

A forlorn notion to bring some pleasure
Life is for living and not for hating
When we hate we lose a part of ourselves
To a distorted view created by tactlessness
Rise up, we pray, to live beyond measure

We must lose the fear that holds us back
Once we see the corrupt lies beneath the sky
We cannot lock ourselves away in despair
When the truth shows itself in awkward places
When they know we see through the façade
We can live not relinquishing to the big lie

THE IGNOMINIOUS DECEITFUL

There has never been a truthful tale
Spoken from the lips of a politician
A police officer inept in their role
A Social Worker who lives
For reaching targets
Just so their next budget
Is honoured – or indeed
Increased
Not
A care they share for the vulnerable
Never a true reflection
Of any given
Situation
They tell us only what they need to
When overall they seek only to deceive us
But we the knowledgeable
The world never wants to believe us
A little truth
Is all that we seek
Still we are the meek
The untitled
The ignorant
The pacifists who sit back and allow
The leaders of our services
The trysts of our world broken
For a mere token
Of gratuity
Found in the laws of power and glory
We choose to believe
What we conceive
To be the true vision of Earth
What we falsely represent
Is our past
Future
Moreover, present hopefulness

That the lie we're being sold
Will never, to our ears, be told
We don't want to hear
What we can make disappear
Way above this
Stratosphere

BREAKING SOLITUDE

Ever knowing with something else
If hope becomes you
Waking up in
A never-ending river
Of dreams that multiply
Of hope that crucifies
Shall heaven seek a disingenuous soul tonight
Sought for love renewal
Given for all the losses we incurred in the end of judgment
Conclusion still has to come for you

A pitiful sight of desolation when love
Leaves you
In a state of cryogenic emotional unbalance
Lost
To the darkness
Without the ability to function
Unable to feel as if you belong
Maybe you don't feel you deserve to be
In a world where painful memories, tears and hate
Engulfs the beauteous side of your soul
Which leaves you bitter and resentful
Hating yourself
Each thought becomes morbid
Each day a struggle to stay alive
Locking yourself behind closed doors
Of solitude and depressive episodes
Where is the love that meant so much
Nothing breaks the cycle of death
Of the soul, if not, of the body

There are better things to do
Than lose yourself to a world of sadness
The malignant actions of those
Less in control of their own hearts and minds
Promiscuous in their thoughts
Of bringing pain and suffering to ease their own
Which never works, as it is returned tenfold
The solitude of lonesomeness

Is futile
When those causing your suffering
Are worth less than two of you alone

THE CRYING WIND

The crying wind of a dying earth
Filters through trees of pestilence
Surrounded by swamps of toxic waste
As rainforests die by the unfailing
Ruinous hand of man

The object of desire is power
Causing destruction in the path
Of the greedy illuminatus fools
Who speak of their role with acidity
Without barely understanding

The world is governed by those
With no altruistic notions for the people
They preside over and ignominious souls
Who feel they have no control to pursue
Their captive heart's true reflections

The earth dies screaming in tortured sequence
Framed in a crime of ignorance and dishonour
Manipulated in a war of self-indulgence
Whilst trying to reflect the blame
Back to the ignorant captives

The fakery voted in office
Time and time again never erodes
Each new governing body brings its own
Lies and manipulation, never recognising
The voices calling out in The Crying Wind

ALWAYS YOURS...

How do I pay tribute
To a love so divine, valiant and wonderful
With words fitting to be written
Only on pages of gold

Through what good deed
Did I deserve my present glory?
Surreptitiously passed onto me
Something heaven never sold

Imagine nature leaping
With joy and not despair
The sick healed indefinitely
As stars, fill the sky
Diamantine in the air
This soft, gentle breeze as lovers walk
We feel enchanted
To be there

Each time you close your eyes
I'll be here by your side
Holding onto you heroically
Leaving you without a care

Memories are made of this
The allure such feelings bring
Reaching out across our world
Through this diamond sky we both share

BRAVURA SONG

It's been so long
Bravura song
Since your melody played inside
The flight has been
So unforeseen
To make such fondness justified
As people change
Things rearrange
In an arduous war of pride
Years of torment
Months represent
Weak in plateau undignified
One star-filled night
She graced my sight
With an image that helped decide
Such fondness true
Cannot undo
What these two hearts have verified
It seemed so wrong
Bravura song
Your tunefulness was placed aside
The discord felt
Lost as I melt
In eyes of fondness rectified

SURRENDER

I hear your voice in the night
Across the miles
Through the barricades
Of pious design

In a stupor I board a reverie train
Contemplate days lost
Lips in secret passion
Life on borrowed time
To an illusory caprice

I SURRENDER

I DREAMT SOMEBODY LOVED ME

Last night – once asleep
I dreamt somebody loved me
Their fingers outlining my face
Kisses – soft and delicate
Sweetened
Like carnation petals
So very gently
Brushing my nose
As my senses
Are drawn to the fragrant bouquet
And captured for posterity

We learn to slow dance
Amidst sexual tracing
Of two bodies becoming one
Born unto lovers erotic dawn
Pleading for more with those eyes
In alluring sensuality
A familiar expression
Exchanged with no words
Spoken
Just a look and a touch
Of warm intimate skin
Laying graceful over mine
Tranquillity
Personified
Fingers locked together
In romantic endeavour
The sun shone – the blue sky
Conducting bird's choir
Blissful
Amorous songs
As morning arrived
I waken to their chorus
To realise

Last night I dreamt somebody loved me
No harm – false alarm

THE OTHER WOMAN

The other woman
Is who I wanted you to be
Not the cold, calculated one
You would show to me

Manipulated by the puppet master
Toying with the strings of my heart
Crassly playing a game
From the very start
The end of forever
Came before we begun
An icy shiver of fear
And it looks like you won
Heartache by the number
One, two, three – and more
Seems the puppeteer
Played this game before

The book fell by the wayside
In twilight moons of fate
Always, always I proceed to find
The other woman before it's too late

She's not the one you showed to me
But the one you pretend to be

SOLITARY MAN

Introverted in the daytime
Lonely nights listening to a mockingbird sing
Over crowds of laypeople

Longing for a mate
To bring a feast of carnality

Full moon on the horizon
Just another night of seclusion

Black bodies the remnants of normality
And here I stand
A solitary man

The sudden smell of burning flesh
Aching all over like it's my own
The rain and wind work together
So I don't putrefy

Waking up in a minefield
A sequestered soldier on patrol

One foot on the firing mechanism
One step off – I'm forsaken no more

RAINBIRDS

We breathe the wind as merely air
Raindrops of a sensual dream
Inspiration comes from somewhere
Two young rainbirds drifting upstream

Basking in the opulent flair
Held in the joy of nature's theme
No shelter found the deluge there
At peace within this weathergleam

No rendering of solitaire
Delight in the journey extreme
Escape together whereso'er

Fly my beloved – I declare
Our shepherd is this love supreme
This heart becomes your doctrinaire

SHOULD I WRITE HER A POEM

A look so sultry from a print
Shall enchant the dreams tonight shares
Her words have grace with just a glint
Of verselet that express her affairs
This picture shows a gentle hint
Of all the feelings her heart wears

I can't quite claim that love shone its ray
My heart fluttered – her allure hooked
My soul in every likely way
Such wispy romance where I have looked
My thoughts extremely fond today
My pen has a kind poem booked

She gave to me a delicate smile
I'm rapt – as her charm fascinates
I'd like to know more in a while
To do just as my instinct states
So these meek words which I compile
I hope with ease she translates

THE EYES HAVE IT

So much sadness
Behind those eyes
Where tears are afraid to fall
Where freedom has no way to call
So many echoes
Inside that mind
Which haunt your every thought
Hide abstrusely in someone you're not
The echoes are the father
You begin to understand
The Father is the life
When no one else is at hand

It's a pain-filled
Armageddon
Exclusive to your heart and soul
Sentience challenging control
Assertion unheard
Quietly calling
You try to turn a deaf ear
Never sure if you want to hear
Your translucent self
Offering the choice
Of somewhere else you'd rather be
Than wrapped up in your misery
And rueful taciturn sounds
In your world of emptiness
Ingest this comprehension
Satiate your hungriness

A CRUSHED DISPOSITION LEFT BY WEAKNESS

Love is a mystery
History is a guide
Tormented hearts
Lustful
In mind and body
For the radiance
Inside
That once prominent feeling
Dwelling in a lacklustre life
The magnificent soul
You created
And took
Away
And I love you so
Much more each passing day
Even as I try to forgive
Forget
To let the days live free
Of thoughts of you
So I may die
Guiltless
And liberated
The memories remain
The heart bears no restraint
Smiling at the revelry, we satiated
A broken heart seems a rather modest way to go
I would know
I *would* know

TIMELESS

Warm summer's daybreak has begun
We didn't feel the cold last night
Persuasive eloquence as one
Knowing where you are in starlight
In the gold of the morning sun
The day goes by so very slow
We know that we are so
Chosen

O how I have lingered so blue
To kiss your lips and touch your hand
In dreams I can always tell you
Here in my heart you understand
The clock ticks on, as it will do
Time seems to stand so very still
Insecurities will
Accrue

But in a moment I can smile
When I remember all we are
Even though we're apart a while
We're wishing under the same star
Feel the love across every mile
An elegant dovetail feather
Till we are together
Gentile

And it is going to be our bliss
We offer everything we can
Amazing love leaves us speechless
And of the times we almost ran
We thought of all we both would miss
And sailed on in this love we know
Then made both our hearts grow
Timeless

<u>Otto Dual</u>

OTTO DUAL

DJ MacDonald created the Otto Dual form in 2003. The form consists of eight line stanzas, with two and eight being a theme hence the Italian 'Otto Dual'. It has a rhyming pattern to.

The stanzas are:

8a

8b

8a

8b

8a

8c

6c

2a

The numbers represent syllable count, the letters the rhyme pattern. The general idea is to end each stanza in two syllables (if you are very clever a one word syllable ending)

PANTOUM

The next poem is a "Pantoum" and where the book takes its title. It was originally a Malayan form, later adapted by the French. Many struggle with this form, due to its repetitiveness. Lines 2 and 4 become lines 1 and 3 in the subsequent stanza. With a variant theme linked to the final stanza, which uses line 1 and 3 from the first Stanza reverses them and puts them in line 2 and 4.Personally I love writing this form, see what you think.

SIMPLY MUSING

Take my heart as I am simply musing
I take a picture of your tender soul
As inspiration, you offer so much
My pen seems to know well the way to flow

I take a picture of your tender soul
Hold it for posterity in my mind
My pen seems to know well the way to flow
When I hold your love close to my heart

Hold it for posterity in my mind
The first time I shall kiss your sweetened lips
When I hold your love close to my heart
And your exotic body wakes my morn

The first time I shall kiss your sweetened lips
As inspiration, you offer so much
And your exotic body wakes my morn
Take my heart as I am simply musing

Pantoum

PAINTED LADY

On your leaves of thistle and hollyhock
You emerge from a small egg of pale green
Lime, yellow, purple, black caterpillar
Moulting your skin from your webbed nest unseen

Your chrysalis splits lady butterfly
As you pump the blood throughout your four wings
Inflating them as you hang there to dry
Absorbing nature, as to you, it sings

Painted lady you can soon fly away
Sipping sweet thistle and clover nectar
Find your mate to procreate the same way
The feel of nature be your protector

In your short life, you will have seen it all
Started the cycle to begin again
In two weeks of birth you receive the call
You're needed for a special purpose then

Your splendour forever reproducing
Our memory flows, as you're kept alive
Through the mate you're so keen on seducing
Born only to ensure your species survive

Your elegance the essence of nature
Your warmth as bright as any summer sun
Your breath-taking; amazing colours shine
Remaining blissful when your life is done

POCKETFUL OF RAIN

I shall not disgrace myself
Nor will I be put to shame
When I speak my mind
With unfailing courage
Through intensified citation
This heart and soul will be held
In respect whether through life
Or through death, now and always
As far too many people
Hold a pocketful of rain
When I die for freedom with certainty
I see my death as a gain
To the fame of eternity

If however, I am to live
A life in the flesh down here
I shall be fruitful
Essential for the sake of us all
My burning desire is to be free
To leave this world and set forth
For something proud to be true
I am hard pressed between two worlds
But to remain an earthly concern
Is far better so we may be heard
Against all that resonates repression
I shall stay so we may promote
The joy of believing
That me and you will triumph
In all manner of life
Standing firm and united in spirit
Striving side by side
Contending with the deluge
It takes one single mind to fight
To not be frightened by the power
The adversity we face
Is a clear sign of deliverance
From the rain
So we may hold with reverence

A pocketful of sunshine again

PERFECT SYMMETRY

We share the same love
Living in harmony
One conscientious mind
Two hearts in perfect symmetry
As one in purpose
The true spirit of love supreme
Held in highest esteem
Of humility

Humbled as we have obeyed
In the presence of tenderness
Creating the power
Energising the desire
Of pleasure and delight
Stars shining out in a dark world
The word of life unfurled
As pure love

We shall not live our life in vain
We hope and trust in each other
Complimentary tender souls
Rapt in our share of it
Devoted interests
From the two hears love borrows
Seems it really ends our sorrows
To welcome us home

WHEN THAT DOOR OPENS

I thank God in celebration of you
My desired joy in every prayer
From the first time we met until today
Your compassion and love comes shining through
I am confident of the perfection
Of a love that can never ever die
When that door opens, make it all your life

It's something to feel this way about you
You have captured me in your heart of love
I hold you in my heart sharing this grace
Even as I'm locked in my own prison
I pursue you with my tender mercy
Your love will bring greater understanding
I will be waiting when that door opens

Someday I pray you'll learn to draw me near
To recognise the real value of we two
With pure, unsullied, blameless, sincere hearts
Who have stumbled; fallen to the fear
Unbound or fulfilled in the fruits of
The glory of love we once recognised
When that door opens forever inside

I want you to know what has happened
Can only help to renew the belief
That the imprisonment in which we serve
These chains will fall when the word of love speaks
With freedom true to the loyal spirit
No more bitterness from these falling chains
When that door opens proclaiming true love

What does it matter that we are apart
So long either way in honesty
We will be together hereafter
I know this will work out through and any
Love will turn out in bountiful supply
With persistent expectation and hope

We will be together when that door opens

WHEN ADAM CHOSE TO FOLLOW EVE

When Adam chose to follow Eve
I wonder if he would believe –
The demoralization he'd create
The world today can illustrate
With war and crime and economic crush
Life is so erratic – everyone's in a rush –
Our Lord once said many religions would run
In the end there'd be proved of Gods – but one
The cantankerous, splenetic world we live in
All because our first chose to give in –
I wonder if his thoughts conveyed
The consequences of God's Word disobeyed
As the serpent said in sweetest voice
Then Eve offered Adam that same choice
To eat fruit from the forbidden tree
Just what effect that would have on you or me –
We didn't choose to deviate
From the Garden of Eden – liberate –
When Adam steered from His plan –
Did he condemn each woman, child, and man?

LOVING YOUR TOUCH

Titillation
In the midnight hour –
A deeply sensuous moment
Your perfectly toned naked body
Laying close to mine
The temperature of the night
Is tepid
Though the heat of two as one
Brings everlasting
Gentleness
Of a new depiction

You lay on one side
Curved away
Anticipating the touch of my hand
Drawing my skin near
Our lovemaking is soft
And sincerely
Amatory
The candles seem to dim
Long before we ever do

I lean forward
To kiss your finely shaped shoulder
I pull you close
When I hear a sigh
Tenderly
I think I am glad
That in this ever-changing world
There will always be
We two – and
This night
To commit to memory

OPUSCULE, OH POET

Opuscule, oh poet!
There's something to be said – that's

Opuscule, oh poet,

I observe all I see
Painting pictures with the words I pen;

Reach out so someone can feel
And know it.

The mysteries of life are
A creation of their own.

Where does this enchantment come from?
That echoes every soul.

Each line a lifelong scar
Poetry - it's who we are!

Opuscule, oh poet!

RETRIBUTION ON THE PERSONIFICATION OF DEATH

The heart,
The reaper sees it
As a misconceived lie
Amassing smoke of darkness
Black like a starless, moonless sky
Covering a valley of skeletal remains
Emotionally inept to see through
The horned one's delusion
Ripping at the tendons
Like a rabid dog
Tearing at a bloodied rag
As the devil gloats
Thinking he has me
Right where he wants me
The game is played in reverse
I find the strength and energy
To overcome all emotive weapons
That may form against me
The smile is erased from his lips
I am the last man standing
Laughing in the face of adversity
I will not be slain!
I am protected!
I am not a victim!
I am triumphant!
More than a survivor
My soul may cry in secret
My eyes may run tears
Weeping bitterly
But downfall is never an option
In this life

Woman DJ

The inner sadness
She'll rarely display
Through ephemeral voice –
Friends unaware of
The adulation she craves
Set free – through these airwaves

Private indiscretions
Encapsulated
Narcissistic pursuits
There to remind her
She's so much better than she knows –
As the fable grows

A sassy veil of low self-esteem
Her mulish front secretes
Commitment is a theme
She will evade
Never to confess
Her path of loneliness

Rock and roll will sell her soul
Losing herself in the music
She won't believe in heroes
To rescue her someday
The lights on – no-one's home
At night – when she's alone

BLUE FUNK

Where did you go, my love?
Dispersing in the night like
A fading star
Who once shone like a diamond
Fizzling out
Echoing through the dark

My soul is lost
With ergonomics in transition
As my potency is
Palpable by creed
Such is true belief

The prowess of heart dissipates
In each passing day through fear
Despite methodical hope
That one day – *one day*
We shall meet in the bloom of June

Self-abasement
In dole melancholia
Will be lifted
When you come back to me

EMPTY ROOM

They disregard my daily struggle
The constant fight to survive
In a world, where kindness or decency
Respect or community spirit
Has almost entirely dissipated
Gradually people have grown fond
Of mockery, profiteering and hatefulness
We have prohibited – *love*
We have dispensed with freedom
A world where the eagerness
To disparage and destroy our neighbours
Friends or colleagues seems second nature
A world where the innocent die in their droves – daily
Where friends become enemies all too easily
This is a world, in which
We are expected to belong

Whereas I have become disconnected
Alone in the hateful campaigns
That serve only to discredit or rescind
I no longer want to be here
I can no further cohabitate
Where destruction of moral values
Impress the weak, cruel and small-minded
That same group of like-minded people
Who push me into darkness

Each day I live
With death a constant thought
I close the door on this world
For fear I may become just like them
How do you articulate
You have lost the will to live?
Emotional pain engulfs
The heart and mind
How do I explain – I live in an empty room

I've always believed if you have to
Ask why someone is depressed
Why they live in such obscurity
You are truly not the person
To help with or deal with their life
You should not make decisions
For them in any form
As the war against the opaque mind
Can only be fought and won – *alone*

LIFE YOUR OWN WAY

I look to give you all my life
Treat you like a princess
Love you like a King's wife
It is all pretence
To fulfil your need
You plant the seed
As I draw near, further away you shove
As I remember
You gave me none of
The things you think you're above
Put me down; keep me keen
When all I want is your love

There is never any intention
To fulfil those hopes
Your played by your invention
A manipulative game
To drive me insane
With nothing to gain
You hide behind a shy smile
As I remember
A saint to a sinner
Deception is your style
You leave me counting the cost
Of the heart that you beguile

There is no rhyme or reason, only your goal
The only thing you give is
Torment to a gifted soul
One day, you'll find yourself
Left destitute
By your ineptitude
You like to toy all day
As I remember
You always want
Life your own way
But for that which we want the most
There's always a price to pay

THE POET MAN

Are we believing
What The Poet Man say
When he brought us
The Starlite Café
Loves lost – loves gained
With sweet inquire
Many of us write
With our hearts on fire

Did we ever consider
From where he came
To touch our lives
And never be the same
There are many moments found
Using weighted dice
We're playing to shine
Thanks to his self-sacrifice

Are we hearing
What The Poet Man say
Even though – he's not
Here with us today
The light was dimmed
From his ailing eye
The world will turn to chaos
When doves cry

We must hide our sorrow
Our poetic works – pen on
In the name of our dearly loved
Even though he's gone
And yet I wonder why
Oh why, must we pretend
Only Albert and God know –
In the end

SORDID MIRRORS

Lead me from this forsaken – stygian room
The shadows on the walls often entomb
A discerning ambience of dark days
Such onerous views I would paraphrase
Words and pictures concocted in my mind
A true reflection wholly undefined
Sordid mirrors reveal this house of pain
Fencing me in – making me feel insane
I look back accepting from where I came
And my refusal to allow this stage to maim
I now walk a land of fulfilling dreams
No lingering of my darkened mind's screams
I'm privileged to be where I am today
Hitherto I would lock myself away
Dancing in rainbows – sordid mirrors told
I stepped out into the light from the cold
Disinterred rhapsodizing that won't be pigeonholed

WHAT'S THE DIFFERENCE?

An erstwhile smile of judgment
A former ally leering
In stark contrast to the pride it stood for

Cold and unfeeling like winter squall
Eroding laudable thoughts

Within a mind so bitter
There can be no greater unity

A nuance of contemplation
No transcendental knowledge exists

A soul where deliberation
Waves its feral finger
To whitewash the innocence

UP AND DOWN

The equity of time
Twists in the heart
Like a tormented demon
Spending each minute
Torturing the spirit
As a heinous crime
The mind forever questions
That of which it has no control
The echoes resonate
Through the darkness
As you purse your lips and bite

Nervousness seems natural
A controlling Emperor
There's a terror locked inside
To which there is no key
Up and down the mood goes
Until you isolate yourself
To withdraw from reality
The intensity of the soul
Seeks only to peel away
Your outer layers to expose
What lies beneath
Even though you wish for no one
To be acquainted with this thing
You do not understand
You cannot explain
You wouldn't know where to begin
To reveal the hidden horror
Time cannot seem to erase

LYING HEART

The first of many moments
Lost to the virginity of the soul
Indecisive games are played
With adeptness for no goal
Talk of forever; always on the edge
Of the dark side of integrity's pledge

The mountains I must climb up
To recover the loss to me you borne
There's never any question
I'd be cheated and forlorn
Which is exactly the way you left me
In a mangled mess where you bereft me

From a whisper to a scream
It feels as if I'm dying more each day
I'll never be good enough
No matter how much I pray
Defeated and useless is how I feel
This life I've been sold is an unfair deal

I cannot support the people
Who need me to stand up for them the most
I cannot even function
To sadness my mind plays host
There's never any reason now or then
To ever make me feel human again

And so I'm cotton candy
Sickly sweet and bad for your existence
No one will get close to me
Better to keep your distance
I'm damaged goods, my black heart tainted
Leave right now before we become acquainted

I feel like I am dying
With no purpose, hope or dreams to follow
If you're trying to reach me

You will find I am hollow
You drained every ounce of life from my heart
I hope, for you, it was worth tearing it apart

SETTLE DOWN

My fondness flows like a river
To your calm sea – *oh sweet amour*
I talk of days so fine
To your heart in time
As the sun is sinking –
If I want you
Is it a crime

Softly in the dusk, golden light
You're singing – *fruitfully*
My heart is heavenly crowned
My eye shed a tear
By the moon – *echoes ringing*
Far apart
Yet – held so near

We'll wander together
In the evening's anticipation
It has never brought me
A dream as sweet as you
I love the look of what you're thinking
I will go home
If you come too

MY SWEET ANGEL

And so….
She met her fate
In wounded clouds of heaven above
Like a bird flies to migrate
As I keep the memories, I love
Also if I am permitted to dream a lie
Time will be on our side
To offer a magnanimous goodbye
Inasmuch as I'm unsatisfied
There are no more tears to fight back
Despite the regrets that persevere
They make me an insomniac
I'll assume these grow year to year
They presume to always keep you on my mind

I imagine you fly the blue serene
My sweet angel indefectibly refined
Soaring the azure gracefully pristine

LOVE WIDE AS AN OCEAN

Deep crystal blue ripples
Like a shroud around our unclothed bodies
Enveloped in perpetuity's supple molten lips

Naked skin on skin swathed beneath the brine
Absorbing the merging of our souls as one

We indelibly focus on the future we pledged to ourselves
Indiscriminate uninhibited exertion captured our caprice of desire

Whilst the spiritual arousal of our minds as we sleep
Creates picturesque images of waves cleansing our virtue

I long for an enduring look far from the surface of those emerald eyes
So therefore wonder will you meet me tonight
Where love can span the ocean wide to unite us?

FANTASY IN OVERDRIVE

Explore and feel
All that makes sensuous rejoice
Explore and feel
Your deep desires to me reveal
Let me hear your ecstasy voice
Let the fantasy be your choice
Explore and feel

Love me madly
Teach me your all in everyway
Love me madly
If you're a bad girl I will gladly
Help make a deal that you can pay
Let me feel every word you say
Love me madly

Fall into me
Much more intensely than before
Fall into me
I'll show you how good bad can be
See I'm just nasty to the core
I'll pay your highest price and more
Fall into me

Let love fly free
A fantasy in overdrive
Let love fly free
Intoxicating you and me
Pleasures to prove we are alive
Ultimate wishes to survive
Let love fly free

BELLEND BARRY BOARDS A BUS

Today here's what I saw
Bellend Barry board a bus
To destinations known only to him

His ever-expanding waistline like
The biggest balloon I ever saw

He had chocolate on his chin
Egg yolk dripped down his working shirt

He snaps the cost of the journey fare
To anyone who travels there

The day's eatables on display
As his bus chugs and chugs away
You can't help but think – how boorish!

I SHALL BE GLAD OF YOUR PASSING

Madam (Or Sir) you are pitiful
If not subjectively hypocritical
Of wanton scandal spoken
From the tongues of the
Amorous or sexually overt
Who cry alone
When at home
Because they are so consistently sated in
Malefic contagion of the soul
That spreads like wildflower
Across my intestines
At each juncture of our contact
As ill-fitting as it may seem
I may choose to dance on your grave
Rejoice in the news of your death
By the glory of our Lord
Then again, I may not rejoice
As I may not be fit to judge
But the almighty God of us all
Most absolutely resolutely shall
May He have mercy on your soul
Even if I feel
He has no business doing so
Still…

I shall be glad of your passing
And smile

ASSIDUITIES

Sweet river of calmness
Fills my soul
Cascading a fervent heart
To taste a ductile kiss

Serenity embraced
You could not supplant
An infinite blessing
Upon lonely lives
Where the sun and moon
Of seclusion drift

Sweet river of calmness
Flow still
Flow still

PERFECT SYMMETRY

We share the same love
Living in harmony
One conscientious mind
Two hearts in perfect symmetry
As one in purpose
The true spirit of love supreme
Held in highest esteem
Of humility

Humbled as we have obeyed
In the presence of tenderness
Creating the power
Energising the desire
Of pleasure and delight
Stars shining out in a dark world
The word of life unfurled
As pure love

We shall not live our life in vain
We hope and trust in each other
Complimenting tender souls
Rapt in our share of it
Devoted interests
From two hearts love borrows
Seems it really ends our sorrows
To welcome us home

DO NOT FADE LIKE SUNSET

How will I find my destiny?
I do not know which path to choose
I analyse with scrutiny
Life; in an effort to diffuse
The obsessive ignominy
To relive a time that is gone
We see it captured on
Cine

A movie that plays in my mind
Screaming and hollering like babes
Digging like a bully unkind
Till the pinnacle of my soul fades
With only a black hole to find
So hard to override these now
Such feelings disavow
Unbind

So tied to a lingering past
That desecrated my whole life
Anger and bitterness – avast!
Do not tie me down with such strife
Spirit within break the spell cast
As I am made for greater things
Spanned like Albatross wings
Sunfast

~ Otto Dual ~

THE SWEET ALLURE

Morning draws close to
Solitary beats of a languid heart
The expectation of you will avow
Tender touches
A delicately painted work of art
With one voice - we composed somehow

The pining comes
Finding you the most central part of me
How I wish I could hold you near
In loving embrace
Just the way we two forever should be
Until that day, I will have you cradled here

Of you I will daydream my time away
Until I have you by my side to stay
The sweet allure I hold will never stray

Romantic notions
Fulfil my every thought so completely
The life we will lead guides a future so bright
In perfect harmony
Honey sweet sound of love soothing dulcetly
The mellifluousness of our hearts beat in the night

The promises
Which we owe each other to make come true
In time, will be something for us to achieve
A devoted oath
Which pledged our hearts together wedged with glue
Those golden moments of forever ours to retrieve

Of you I will daydream my time away
Until I have you by my side to stay

The sweet allure I hold will never stray

BEYOND LOVERS

Beyond the moon rediscovers
The true hearts of modern lovers

The joy of the heart overflowed
The promises of such lovers

In the sky as the moonbeam glowed
Delight comes for loyal lovers

The moonlight in darkness shadowed
The shining love of true lovers

The stars made good on pledges owed
Love rains down on star-crossed lovers

~ Ghazal ~

FLY WITH THE WIND

Fly with me to the Earth's ends
feel the wind flow on your face
Embrace me like no other
I your dove you are my wings
We can fly seeking with clear vision
our destiny to be one

~ Sijo ~

LIFETIME OF THOUGHTS DEPARTED

The pen, the poet, the man
Wrote a lifetime of thoughts departed
You picked up the pieces
The confidante I always wanted
You had me cradled
I would be sheltered
You never afraid to take me home
When I'm alone in obscurity

Today, you make me see that I am vulnerable
It is something I must embrace
You win a little; lose a little
Nevertheless, you are my haven
You bring me to a sanctuary here

You emboldened me and gave me tenacity where I needed it
Your angels brought solace to me in
The sunless daylight
When the darkness swathes
Face down in nescience
When nothing made sense

I turned away
For so long I was away from your duteous fold
You received me home
I knew I belonged

I am unfettered
I can reveal every part of my being
Through opulent words that you accede to

JUST A WARRIOR LIKE YOU

Life plays like a roulette wheel of bane warfare
Preoccupied hallucinatory
Confusion – waking up in a minefield
Of frayed dissident faces

How are they to understand?
If I do not know why I'm here fighting wilfully
For the glory of my country
Unswerving – faithful – a *dedicated* guard

All I know is I can help bring a quality of life
Something long since emancipated
Amidst evil tyranny

Defender of the earth – countryman true
You say I'm a hero retaining liberation
I'm just a warrior like you – life's *mortal* soldier

ACID TOWN

Paint the imagery
Scenes of unrepentance
Walk with me to Acid Town
Walk through the valley
Of the shadow of death
A place that turned me so bitter
Ignominiously
Derivative of
Impenitent sin
Scowling through darkness
Like a rabid
Dog biting his own flesh
With piquant tongues
You are shame
You have no concept of life
You ignoramuses
What goes around comes around
In Acid Town

DESIRE

Desire the ocean
That carries us smoothly to
Visions of stillness

Desire the green grass
Where lovers fantasize as
They lay together

Desire love's heaven
In a marriage of true minds
Our souls born as one

Desire a blue sky
Sublime castles in the air
Making dreams come true

Desire a rainbow
Luminous colours of life
The riches unfold

~x~ Haikus ~x~

THE SKY DIES CRYING

Breaking silent echoes over the mountains
Ripples in the water of musical fountains
Gone in the night a shadow cast
A legend begins his story shows
A fondness of his art indelibly grows
The love his art increases *en masse*
There upon the snowy hills angels descend
To capture the soul of our journeying friend

A Texan son's cowboy hat and leather boots
Cascade with guitar riffs his seed bears fruit
In each tune how he made that guitar dance
A mystical figure impressions our minds
In his music our hearts durably binds
How he made his mark by works not merely chance
Soldier of fortune lost in a Texas flood
With rhythm in his heart and blues in his blood

If the sky dies crying for all that is lost
Until the earth dies screaming we're counting the cost
He is rockin' with an electric gypsy today
Two guitars with two guitar heroes who needs more
When I am called home some truly fateful way
I hope to be front seat at the concert on show
You have to admit, what a way to go

As the rain falls in a crescendo on my rooftop
In the distant echo the strumming guitars don't stop
I picture myself there in a moment of spiritual release
Echoing through the transcends of time and space
Like an open gateway to another worldly place
The legend lives on and the music will never cease
For the master genius at work portrays his art
So that we on this earth can take it all to heart

WHISKEY IN THE GUITAR

I hear it on the radio
That old song, 'Whiskey In The Jar'
Playing in digital audio
The sound of thunderous guitar

I rock through each empty bottle
Like a true mosher in the pit
Turn up the volume full throttle
Classic rock you can't beat it

Am I truly playing the song
Or is the song playing me
To dance alone is weirdly wrong
As my drunken mind cannot see

If the instrument was whiskey
The bottle could not play a tune
It appears to be rather risky
If I fail to stop rockin' soon

No one sees it is safe to assume
I suspect they can't see just yet
The more I actually consume
The merrier I seem to get

It truly makes me want to sing
But still, I really ought to stop
If whiskey were a guitar string
I wouldn't touch a plucking drop

DREAM THE DREAM

Words flow onto paper in cascades
As they run into your dreams
Your oceanic profundity
These images you create
Poetic words mediate
As they rain back down on me

Days aligned with elegiac delusion
Pass by in portraits of you
Correlating telepathically
Talking hour upon hour
Transcendently entwine our
Souls emphatically

The stars are far away and diamonds cold
I've tried to touch them for you
Long ago – I *slow danced* with someone
Got used to dancing apart
Here I write from the heart
Of you in comparison

Afraid to see how alike we are
The futile works we pursue
Have changed – we pretend we don't see it
Looking far across the ocean
Hold close this emotion
Don't dream the dream – *let's be it*

SOMETIMES LIKE BUTTERFLIES

Evade the
Wind, enormously at ease
Bouncing away through all the
Beauteous
Things around me

Therefore, it is plain to see
Exactly where I would be
Flying; gliding; drifting
Joyous, soulful and free
Wings flattering delicately
In the sun

Mine enemies eyes turn
Away in jealous disdain
As I see the world
Through the eyes of God
Proud to believe in Him
Proud to conceive through Him
We have lost the way of natural earth

DREAMS ARE JUST THE SAME

A fusion of colours
Borne of the mind like luminous rainbows
Reaching far across the sky
Set in a backdrop of ice blue
Still the more I reach out
In each fluffy white cloud that passes
I see the peace of my heart and
The piousness of spirit I long for
As it comes back to the love, we share
Which is as distant as the sun that shines
Through an infinite universe
Whose power is as weak as my mind
In search for what I cannot have

I walk the streets where I once lived
Even though they are no longer around
In a metaphysical world
Created in my idle place
Since you have been gone, these dreams remain
Musing on devotion lost
I dream so I may be with
You in reverie

LOVE IS AN INSANE GAME

The hopeless entities
Of our love remains in limbo
The sanctimonious
Irony, scathingly poignant
We are lost
We are never free
There is no escape from the world of pain
We both go through in perpetuity
Ignoring the signs
Sent to us spiritually
Telling us that we should be together
Like a cold January frost
We live in our world of obligations
Morally susceptible
To the tricks of our minds
Which leave us feeling soulless
How inept
How utterly ridiculous
We feel the need to prolong the torture
With those who will never fulfil our needs
Well played
My insalubrious folly

SLOWLY

Slowly
Walk my way
Come to me baby –
Hold me like that
Draw real close with a touch
Feel the heat burning over us
Much too much
The music starts – the stars shine bright
And this is our night
So dance with me
Real slow
Touch me baby
Real soft
Kiss me baby
So wet
As we dance –
Slow

Slowly
Night passes
Soaked in desire
Embracing by candlelight
Momentum of the glowing moon
On a darkened warm night
The more we try
To see if this is heaven – *I'm falling*
Ecstasy is calling
Love uncontrolled
Real slow
Touch me baby
Real soft
Feel me move
So free
Hooked on you –
Slow

WHY DOES A MAN HAVE TO BE STRONG

Only in my dreams, I turn you on
Here for a moment then you're gone
Is it an act or illusion?
As we indulge in this fusion
The absence of security
Gives me perspicuity
In my thinking that just maybe
I happen to miss my baby
When I can't set the world on fire
I am crying over desire
I should make a little movement
To give my mind some peace improvement
Because there's loving in these eyes
I'm stupid cupid in disguise
Had some bad love that went so wrong
For the good I've been waiting so long
Why does a man have to be strong?

CRESTFALLEN

If you're under
The impression I will abandon you
You'll get to know me better than that

If you think that I will desert you
When you are pleading on bended knee
You'll get to know me better than that

That is one thing
I would not do
If you need to shed some tears
For some lost – lonely – Confusing life
I'll wipe them all away

If you could see deep into me

When you are crestfallen
I will cradle you in my arms
When you are feeling
Desensitized
I'll be there
Right by your side

You'll get to know me better than that

When you are forlorn
Can't get back on your feet
I will show you
You're so much better than you know

You'll get to know me better than that
If everything …
… is an illusion
You cannot see

I will find you
I will bring you home
Girl, you'll get to know me better – than that

THE DAY IT RAINED FOREVER

All we rely on are the raindrops
Tiny crystal terms of goodbye
A constant rainfall never stops
In her words I'm left high and dry
Lonely boy blue on the housetops
Sees some people in love go by
Don't look under stormy weather
Love's gone and it rained forever

Remember the world in your hands
Bringing the dreams you need to know
And if someone else understands
Forget me in mood indigo
You won't care life has other plans
Love follows you wherever you go
These gifted hearts are not so clever
In foolish days that rain forever

I am to be melancholy
Just let me revel here alone
Locked away my world thoroughly
Love's true spirit having flown
We crossed this path naturally
Devotion left once it was shown
A deluge on the realm of never
Today – it's going to rain forever

ETHEREAL LOVE

Serendipitously we are
So good together but – no good apart
I seem to sense *intrinsically*

When you need me the most
And that time seems to be now

I receive your ethereal
Messages

Which call out in the night
Dictum to my intangible soul
Hold me – care for me – *love* me

HOW WINTER KILLS

Blue as the sky
How it used to make me feel so rich

Pitiful dispiriting
Now when I see the colour blue
It reminds of things I should do – *again*

Echoes inside my mind that I do not want to hear
I want to turn a deaf ear
My heart has turned to stone
Inside the stone broke my hourglass
Now I'm blue as the colour of misery – *globule of angst*

So if the sand can't reach the bottom
How am I meant to die
If time won't run out on this godforsaken – burden laden
World that we all live in
I guess it is true – *pain becomes me*
Spring doesn't seem to bring its end

Let the Robin trill
The green rashes grow
Let heaven open up and shine
Its celestial splendour on us
While winter marches to a close – as an ending comes
It brings a new and hopeful beginning
Life is funny like that
It takes you by surprise when you
Least expect it has anything
Even if – it doesn't make your soul sing

However, you can still yearn for
The heart that should belong to you
Even if its tangible touch and kisses are all gone
Memories

Demean you in dejection
The summer of love no longer shines in the gold of the sun
It is the same for every one
You buy a new hourglass
To start the perpetual motion
March brings winter's end, and springs beginning
Soul mates never die in autumn – but – Oh *how* winter kills
Their physical love

THE ACID WELL

The river will not flow
As once it did
The silence of echoes resonates through me
In memory of you
Your day
Where beggars become kings
For dreams, fulfil to glory
In spirit
The Acid Well stirs emotive joy

The future lost
In time's diction
Those all sewn in fate
Death is just the beginning
The doors of the night open
To a world impeccable to this
Where knowledge sought is lessons learned
In a perpetual cycle of all lives lived

Laughter will ring again
If you are taken to the clouds above
As rituals come and go
For death is calling
Eternally we shall meet

FATHER

A distance comes to me
Echoes mirrored through the cracks in time
From where you used to be
Is it a crime
No rhythmic rhyme

The sum of my fears
You differentiate your son
From the despisement that he hears
Love never won
My troubles begun

A rock of ages in the wind
I have nothing left to say
I don't cry at night
Over each petty fight
Memories are not my forte
You were never mine
As I was never your boy
The resentment is fine
As it stole my joy
I have never known joy
I was never your boy

Tomorrow

Where the echoes of tomorrow land
In the withering of a curious mind
Is anyone's guess
You expect nothing less
Than creative spurts of genius
Lost and forlorn
Inevitably born
Just barely developed
Never given a lease of life
Always somewhere in tomorrow

Time is relatively unkind
In the echoes of a curious mind
Comes the madness
Unbearable sadness
The curse of creativeness
An unquiet treasure
Left beyond measure
It turns and turns
It never sleeps but withers away
Echoing somewhere in tomorrow

Final Word …

The concept of human emotion and the art of putting those articulately is difficult for most. At least, difficult to put into words for those you are speaking to in the context of the conversation or the words you wish to put across to your readership. Sometimes words flow like the river to the sea, and then almost immediately the dreaded block comes to mind.

Words are almost certainly life's greatest art form. We should always strive to better our vocabulary or writing skill. It takes some practice. Experience alone, whether in writing or life, does not make you a master of words. Some skill is involved. Like most skills, it can be learned so along as you are following an appropriate path to ensure a viable outcome.

The comedian and actor Kenneth Williams, he of Hancock, Carry On and Round The Horne fame, taught himself a new word from the dictionary every day. He studied the word, researched it for use in sentences, and memorised the meaning. Each day one must push themselves to find ways of learning something they didn't know the previous day. In almost all aspects of learning, I would suggest words, and how to use them properly, is one of the highest attributes to learn and enhance your professionalism or personal life.

It's said that everyone has a novel in them. Perhaps, so if you have ever thought of trying to write, then please do. Practice and learn. The greatness of today's technology means there are many forums online for you to gain feedback from learned writers. Never underestimate the power of the human mind, it's creativity and where to best place that creative outlet. Use your life experience to keep a journal, write short stories, write a novel, or write poetry. Be prepared. I mean prepared to throw away at least half of what you write. Even if it seems OK to you, if it doesn't tick all the boxes for you, abandon it and start again. It's an art. You are never quite right the first time. You are always constantly learning about life, and so should assume, you are always constantly learning about your creative mind, its output, and your writing.

If you are of a mind or brave enough to submit your work for publication or seek representation to do so, make sure you do your research. Ensure whom you are submitting your work to is actually the right agent or publisher. Ensure you know their procedures for submissions. If they don't take unsolicited scripts or novel synopsis, then don't submit. Seek an appropriate agent to represent you and help push you forward. The joy of the Internet is a search engine will help you find everything you need in terms of formats for scripts and novels and information on how to submit to prospective agents etc. Some publishing firms will have submission details on their own webpages. Use them, and submit. Be prepared for rejection. You will get it any number of times. Some of the biggest film scripts and books published in the world got rejected anything up to 20+ times.

Submit, forget about it, and move on to the next work.

However, you intend to use your word skills, for talking, writing, presentations, or life in general, always try to improve. Improving your knowledge brings its own reward, helps boost confidence and brings you a greater mind to take on each day ahead.

You are your own worst enemy. Your mouth is a weapon. It can be deadly. Use your words wisely. Just write and keep on writing if a writer is what you aspire to be. Somehow, with belief, you will conquer all rejection in life and grow confident.

The online sites where you can submit your work, most critiques are people much like yourself an aspiring would-be writer who just wants to reach out and give people the benefit of their experience or creativity. They normally will have some good critique to help improve your style; genuine people do not 'rubbish' your work. No matter how bad it really is, no one should. If you can learn from that experience to improve your skill and adeptness of writing then it's all you really need to get started.

Writing is a great reward; it brings a sense of accomplishment and joy. I truly believe the whole world should write. Learning and improving as you go. If you are not learning new skills, new areas, new words, new styles in your creativity then you are merely standing still. No one wishes to stand still. Everyone must keep moving. If we don't move, we become rigid, stuck, begin to decay or wilt away into nothingness. This is not what you should be doing. Bring yourself some complimentary pats on the back, gather up your pen, write your life experience, if that is what you want to do, write a novel about a subject you are adept in knowledge of, or write poetry.

Everyone must write.

You should write to stay alive, as in you don't breathe air, you die. Your mind can die if it has no congenial outlet for its creative power.

Knowledge is power, read, write, learn, be powerful and enjoy all aspects of life, your way. No one else's…. Just your way, it is the only true way to live.

AUTHOR'S NOTE

DJ MacDonald had previously been a Residential Child-Care Worker, Actor, and professional DJ. He is married with two grown children. He lives on the West Coast of Scotland with his wife, children and dogs Rocky and Harper. As well as writing poetry, he has written several columns for magazines and has many script and novel ideas. One day he may share these.

Poetry has always been a passion. Writing initially as a child then rediscovering this passion late in life. His daughter is a writer of several short stories, mostly related to the supernatural genre.

Electric Thunder Publications

Simply Musing – Poetry Of Life And Love
By
DJ MacDonald

Distributed and marketed by Electric Thunder Productions

Electric Thunder Publications is part of Electric Thunder Productions.

'til we meet again…

Made in the USA
Charleston, SC
06 November 2015